**Innovations in Education Series**
**Edited by Robert J. Brown**

1. Edward J. Dirkswager, ed. *Teachers as Owners: A Key to Revitalizing Public Education*. 2002.
2. Darlene Leiding. *The Won't Learners: An Answer to Their Cry*. 2002.

D0807988

A Note about the Contributors

The editor, Edward J. Dirkswager,
prepared this book with the assistance of
Ted Kolderie, Joseph P. Graba, Stacy Becker, and Kimberly A. Farris.

Other contributors were:
Jon Bacal, Robert J. Brown, Walter W. Enloe,
Thomas W. Garton, Allen Gerber, Harold K. Larson,
Thomas J. Marr, John J. Mauriel, Daniel C. Mott, Ronald J. Newell,
Al Oukrop, Douglas J. Thomas, and James R. Walker

All of the individuals who have contributed to this book have
experience in professional practice organizations and education policy
or practice. They are lawyers, physicians, accountants, consultants,
persons familiar with small businesses and cooperatives, educators,
education policymakers, and educational administrators.

# TEACHERS AS OWNERS

## A Key to Revitalizing Public Education

Innovations in Education Series, No. 1

### Edited by Edward J. Dirkswager
### Foreword by Ted Kolderie

A SCARECROWEDUCATION BOOK
WITH HAMLINE UNIVERSITY

The Scarecrow Press, Inc.
Lanham, Maryland, and London
2002

A SCARECROWEDUCATION BOOK

Published in the United States of America
by Scarecrow Press, Inc.
A Member of the Rowman & Littlefield Publishing Group
4720 Boston Way, Lanham, Maryland 20706
www.scarecroweducation.com

4 Pleydell Gardens, Folkestone
Kent CT20 2DN, England

Copyright © 2002 by Center for Policy Studies

*All rights reserved.* No part of this publication may be reproduced,
stored in a retrieval system, or transmitted in any form or by any
means, electronic, mechanical, photocopying, recording, or otherwise,
without the prior permission of the publisher.

British Library Cataloguing in Publication Information Available

**Library of Congress Cataloging-in-Publication Data**

Teachers as owners : a key to revitalizing public education /
Edward J. Dirkswager, editor.
    p. cm.—(Innovations in education series ; no. 1)
Includes bibliographical references.
  ISBN 0-8108-4372-2 (Cloth : alk. paper)—ISBN 0-8108-4371-4 (Paper :
alk. paper)
  1. Teachers—Professional relationships. 2. Educational innovations.
I. Dirkswager, Edward J., 1938– II. Innovations in education (Lanham,
Md.) ; no 1.
  LB1775 .T379 2002
  371.1—dc21                                  2002004113

♾™ The paper used in this publication meets the minimum requirements of
American National Standard for Information Sciences—Permanence of
Paper for Printed Library Materials, ANSI/NISO Z39.48-1992.
Manufactured in the United States of America.

# CONTENTS

Foreword by Ted Kolderie     vii

Preface     xi

**1**   What Is a Teacher Professional Partnership?     1

**2**   Who Are the Potential Clients of Teacher Professional Partnerships?     7

**3**   What Are the Key Ingredients of Success?     15

**4**   What Are the Options for the Design and Operation of a Teacher Professional Partnership?     29

**5**   What Are the Implications?     51

**6**   EdVisions Cooperative: An Example of a Teacher Professional Partnership     83

**7**   Changing the National Discussion     97

**Appendix A**   Comparison of Legal Structures for Doing Business as a Teacher Professional Organization     103

**Appendix B**   Options for Private Retirement Plans for Teacher Professional Partnerships     111

**Appendix C**   Outline of a Business Plan for a Teacher
Professional Partnership                            115

**Appendix D**   Emerging Model: I.D.E.A.L. Charter School
Cooperative                                         119

**Appendix E**   National Meeting on Teacher Professional
Partnerships                                        123

**Appendix F**   Technical Assistance: Where to Begin        127

Bibliography                                                 139

About the Editor and Contributors                           143

# FOREWORD

The idea is simple—to give teachers the same opportunity as other professionals to work for themselves as partners in a single-specialty or multi-specialty group. To accomplish this, we must abandon the traditional notion that to be a teacher one *has* to be an employee.

But the idea of ownership is not an end in itself. It is instrumental; a means to an end. The end is the creation of high-performing learning communities. The contributors believe that the opportunities and incentives provided by ownership will create new potential for the changes required in teaching if student learning is to improve. Ownership is the key to a complete professional role for teachers.

Ownership is a familiar idea. Many professionals in service and information occupations choose to work in a partnership. They choose ownership rather than employment; they control their own work. There is a dual structure of leadership: they decide the professional questions; the administrators work for them, operating the organization. All of us know professionals who work like this, and many of us deal with their partnerships all the time.

Ownership, however, is not a familiar idea in education. Teachers have always been employees in private as well as in public schools. The administrator of the school is assumed to be the principal. Few of us have any experience with teachers who work for themselves. Few

teachers have any experience working for themselves or being professional leaders, or any thought that they might do so (that is, work for
themselves in teaching: it is not at all uncommon for teachers to work or
to own and run businesses on the side). And because this is the way it
has always been, people tend to think this is the way it has to be: "Whatever is, is right."

But ownership is a conceivable idea for teachers. The partnership
arrangement works—it is common—in other professional occupations.
There is no reason it cannot work in education. Almost certainly the
"employment" arrangement in education is simply historic. Education is
out of step with the rest of the world of work.

Ownership, then, is a feasible idea for teachers and a necessary idea
for education. To open the opportunity requires, mainly, an effort to
adapt the model of the professional partnership to the particular institution of public education or—better expressed in the inverse—to adapt
the institution of public education to the idea of teacher ownership.

All our existing notions about teachers' arrangements—pay and benefits, retirement, and professional roles and responsibilities—are
presently built on the notion of employment. The law assumes employment: we talk about teachers as we do about other employees, being
"hired." New arrangements will have to be designed and constructed so
that we can begin to talk about teachers—as we talk about professionals
in other fields—being "admitted to practice" and about their group being "retained." Adjustments will be needed so that district boards of education can deal with teachers in a professional group, a partnership in
control of and accountable for its professional practice.

This can be done. It will simply have to be done. How it can be done
is the subject of this guide.

We have tried here not to be prescriptive; we have tried to avoid sug-
gesting that there is one right way for a partnership to be organized and
to operate. We have tried to be conscious of the fact that there are a variety of options and—as is true with all institutional innovation—that the
original ideas will change and evolve with experience, and new ideas will
appear. We tried, for example—and readers should try—to think of
ownership as an idea that can be applied to one department of a big high
school or to a program cutting across a whole district with multiple
schools, as well as to a single, whole, discrete school.

Ownership is an important idea for our country as well as for teachers. All our discussions about teachers and teaching and schools—more importantly, all our recent efforts at change and improvement—have been built on the assumption that teachers are employees. And visibly now, the assumption of employment, the denial of complete professional status to teachers, is complicating our efforts to change the nature of schools and to improve learning. It is even possible that the assumption of employment has, in fact, been keeping us from making progress in these efforts at change and improvement.

One example is the current discussion about school leadership. The purpose of the discussion is to improve student learning. But the assumption of employment makes managers, not teachers, the leaders. If teachers are employees, it is hard to think of them as leaders. Yet the evidence suggests that what managers do does not change teachers' practice very much.

In this guide we address how this notion of leadership and several other discussions about teaching and learning might change if the assumption of employment were removed and the questions were rethought with the assumption of ownership. We look at the implications of the ownership idea for state policy leadership, for boards of education and other buyers of what we generally refer to as "school," for students and parents, for teachers and their unions, and for the institutions in which teachers are trained and in which teaching is taught.

Albert Hirschman wrote "We dare not believe in creative discoveries until they have happened" (Hirschman, 1970). So in the guide we also examine a teacher partnership that has "happened" in Henderson, Minnesota, and examine the model of school this partnership has evolved since its beginning in 1994. Chapter 6 describes this partnership, known as EdVisions Cooperative (formally a workers' cooperative, a Chapter 308A organization under Minnesota law), and one of the strikingly different kinds of secondary school it has created, given the opportunities and the incentives provided by ownership.

This teacher partnership and this school have developed within the charter sector of public education, which is open to this kind of new arrangement. But there is no reason for the ownership idea to be confined to the charter sector. It should be available in the district sector, too. The district sector can be adjusted to create an opportunity for teacher partnership in its schools as well.

The idea of teacher ownership arises now in the context of the growing discussion about an "entrepreneurial" model of education. More and more, district boards of education find themselves thinking about getting *out* of the business of "employment"—thinking about contracting for instructional services—as more and more organizations are now getting *in* to the business of running schools.

Until now, people have assumed that organizations contracting to run schools or programs would take a corporate form. This is not a given, however. It is entirely possible for these organizations to form as partnerships of teachers. We simply need to think in new ways. It will not work to try to fit new ideas, such as teacher ownership, into traditional frameworks where people ask traditional questions.

Ted Kolderie

# PREFACE

## THE PROJECT

Efforts to understand and champion teacher professional partnerships (TPPs) began over fifteen years ago. In the 1980s, Ruth Anne Olson developed the idea of teacher ownership of professional practices as a consultant to a Minnesota project entitled Public School Incentives.

Her work was supported by several foundations including Northwest Area Foundation, First Bank System Foundation, F. R. Bigelow Foundation, Medtronic Foundation, and Fingerhut Corporation Foundation. The latter two foundations and Public School Incentives supported the development and production of two 1986 reports: *Private Practice in Public School Teaching. Book I: The Concept, Need and Design,* by Ted Kolderie and *Private Practice in Public School Teaching. Book II: The Experiences of Teachers and School Administrators* by Ruth Anne Olson. Olson worked as a consultant, locating teachers willing to work with a new model and showing them how to do it. She found there was no market at that time for teachers in K–12 education wanting to work on contract.

Senn Brown in Wisconsin became interested in Olson's ideas, and he created the American Association of Educators in Private Practice that carried on the idea for some years before it gradually went another direction. Olson's ideas also stimulated Ted Kolderie at the Center for

Policy Studies in Minnesota to collaborate in the preparation of the 1986 reports, to champion the model, and to look for ways to introduce it to educators and education policy makers. In the early 1990s, he introduced the idea to teachers in the LeSeuer-Henderson School District in Minnesota as they started their design of the charter school, Minnesota New Country Charter School. The group decided to create a professional partnership using the legal form of a worker cooperative, which was well accepted in their rural community.

EdVisions Cooperative, an example of the teacher ownership model, was founded in 1994 when they grew out of those discussions. It worked very well. The success of EdVisions Cooperative encouraged Kolderie to intensify his efforts to get others interested in the model and to explore alternative designs. In early 2000, he met with Tom Vander Ark of the Bill and Melinda Gates Foundation. After a visit to Minnesota New Country School, Vander Ark suggested that EdVisions Cooperative apply for a grant to replicate the model. In the fall of 2000, a $4.4 million grant was given to create fifteen new schools that would also result in ten new teacher ownership organizations.

At this same time, Kolderie and his colleague Joe Graba, then retiring as the dean of the School of Education at Hamline University, asked me, Edward J. Dirkswager, a retired business consultant to physicians and hospitals, to coordinate and direct a project to explore alternative designs and to adapt the model of professional partnerships found in law, medicine, accounting, and other professional groups to public education. The project was sponsored and underwritten by the Center for Policy Studies and Hamline University.

To accomplish the task, Dirkswager assembled a teacher professional partnership steering committee made up of individuals with experience in professional practice organizations such as lawyers, physicians, accountants, consultants, and persons familiar with small businesses and cooperatives, as well as educators and educational administrators. In addition to Dirkswager, Kolderie, and Graba, the active members of the committee included Jon Bacal, Stacy Becker, Robert J. Brown, Walter W. Enloe, Kimberly A. Farris, Thomas W. Garton, Allen Gerber, Harold K. Larson, Thomas J. Marr, John J. Mauriel, Daniel C. Mott, Al Oukrop, Douglas J. Thomas, and James R. Walker. In addition, Ronald J. Newell, Rholan Larson, Lisa J. Wigard, and John Parr provided invaluable assistance to the work of the committee. The editor wishes to express special thanks to Kimberly A. Farris for her assistance in preparation of this guide.

The objective of the steering committee, which met once a month for a year, was to prepare a practical "guide" that would give educators and persons interested in education policy an understanding of what teacher-ownership means, how to go about setting up a teacher professional partnership, why teachers should be interested, what some of the implications are, and an overview of the EdVisions Cooperative experience.

While EdVisions Cooperative has proven that the model can work, it is important to note that it is *one* example, not *the only* example of how it can work. The steering committee's charge was to generalize the experience in other professions and show the various ways in which a teacher-owned partnership can be set up. There are many options for the design and operation of a teacher professional partnership—there is no single right way.

Based on his or her interest and expertise, individual members of the steering committee took the lead in serving as the primary author of the various sections of this guide. Under Dirkswager's coordination, each author worked with other members of the steering committee to develop a draft to present to the entire committee for review and comment.

In September 2001, Hamline University, the Center for Policy Studies, and the Wallace-Readers Digest Funds sponsored a national meeting to elevate awareness of teacher ownership and to bring the idea that teachers could be owners of their professional practice into the forefront of discussion about the future of public education (see appendix E for a description of the meeting and a list of participants.) The meeting provided valuable insights that have been incorporated into the final draft of this guide. The contents of this book, however, remain the responsibility of the editor and the steering committee that assisted in its formation.

The chapters in this guide are structured around several questions: What is a teacher professional partnership? Who are the potential clients? What are the key ingredients of success? How might partnerships be designed and operated? What are the broader implications for those involved in the education sector? What lessons can be learned from EdVisions Cooperative? And where do we go from here?

The appendixes include an outline of the different legal structures for the organization of a professional partnership, an outline of a model business plan, a summary of the retirement plan options available to existing professional partnerships that can be adapted for a teachers' professional group, information on emerging models, and a list of resources for technical assistance in starting a professional partnership.

This guide does not end the need for discussion of teacher partnerships or refinement of the model. Indeed, one of its purposes is to stimulate discussion and critique. We hope the reader will want to engage in a dialogue of the ideas presented here in order to advance thinking about teacher professional partnerships.

## KEY DEFINITIONS

*Teacher Professional Partnership (TPP)*: Throughout the guide we use the term "teacher professional partnership" or "TPP" to refer to the way in which teacher–owners organize themselves professionally and relate to one another. The term is meant to convey the idea of teachers working together in an interdependent, collaborative way to maximize their professional roles; and the term also refers to the idea of a business entity. It is important to note, as we point out in chapter 4, that the actual legal form of the business is not restricted to a partnership model. For example, the business may also be structured as a cooperative. There are a variety of options for the design and operation of a TPP.

*Partner*: We use the term "partner" to describe a teacher–owner. In a cooperative, an owner is called a member. In a law, consulting, or physician practice, the owner may be called a partner, shareholder, or principal.

*Member*: As noted, "member" is the correct legal term for the owners of a cooperative. Therefore, in our discussion of EdVisions Cooperative in chapter 6, we refer to "members" instead of "partners." In other chapters of the guide, we use the term "member" in a broader sense to refer to two types of positions in a teacher professional partnership. Professional partnerships consist not only of owners (partners), but also of associates, who are employees. As we point out in chapter 4, associates may undergo a period of evaluation and may be employed under a temporary status before earning the status of partner. All of the individuals who make up the partnership are referred to as members, but all members may not necessarily be owners.

*Client*: A "client" is a group of persons or entities that purchases educational services from a TPP. Clients are agents for students. A TPP's access to students and revenues results from a relationship with the client, generally by way of a contract. Examples of clients are district school boards, charter school boards, families, and businesses.

# ❶

# WHAT IS A TEACHER
# PROFESSIONAL PARTNERSHIP?

A recent survey on community input into public schools found that most of the public (two-thirds) reported feeling comfortable leaving decisions to "the professionals." Just who are the education professionals the public referred to in this survey? Surely the respondents meant to include teachers as well as administrators. And yet, of all groups surveyed—parents, the general public, teachers, administrators, and school board members—teachers feel the most ignored. Seventy percent of teachers said they are left out of the decision-making process. They believe that their ideas and concerns are not taken seriously by administrators (Farkas, 2001).

As this survey suggests, the professional role of teachers has become a major educational issue. Teachers increasingly feel frustrated and constrained in their efforts to practice their profession. The typical organizational structure of our school systems contains a rigid hierarchy of roles and decision-making power, with teachers firmly positioned at the bottom of this hierarchy. Very simply, teachers are employees, and like most employees in rigid hierarchical organizations, they have a limited range of decision-making powers.

What if teachers, instead of being employees, owned their own professional partnerships? What if teachers formed and ran their own businesses to practice their trade as many lawyers, doctors, and accountants do? What would this "teacher–owner" or "teacher professional partner-ship" model look like?

## WHAT IS TEACHER OWNERSHIP?

Teacher ownership breaks through our customary notions about how teaching is practiced. It recognizes that teachers are professionals and ought to have latitude to practice their trade as other professionals do. Lawyers, doctors, and accountants form and run their own businesses around their areas of expertise. They hire administrators, if necessary, to run the administrative aspects of the business. In this way, they can spend their time using their expertise to its fullest extent.

In a teacher professional partnership, teachers form their own busi-ness to practice the teaching profession. Their "business" is to edu-cate. The responsibility for running the business and achieving success lies with the partners. A teacher professional partnership could be formed as a nonprofit or for-profit enterprise. As subsequent sections of this guide will demonstrate, teacher professional partnerships could be formed using any number of organizational and legal structures, but the end result is always a freestanding, legally constituted business entity.

The formation of a partnership introduces an element of entrepre-neurship into how teaching is practiced. But it need not place monetary gain over the desire to serve, which is a driving motivation of most teachers, just as it can be for people in other professions such as medi-cine and law. The business requirement to perform well is not inconsis-tent with the desire to serve and indeed provides an added incentive for quality teacher performance.

## HOW DO TEACHERS' ROLES CHANGE WITH TEACHER OWNERSHIP?

As owners of a professional partnership, teachers become contractually responsible for the educational services they agree to provide. As a re-sult, they gain control over a variety of decisions that today are typically made by administrators or governing boards. Teacher–owners find themselves with control over and accountability for the design and implementation of the learning program. Teachers with strong ideas about teaching methods or programs have the freedom to develop, implement, and improve upon these ideas, subject only to finding some party who wishes to provide that kind of education for the students for whom it is responsible. The professional partnership determines the appropriate fees to set for its services and then determines how to allocate these fees in a budget among priorities such as member compensation, administrative services supplies, and technology. The partnership takes responsibility for decisions about human resources, such as setting member compensation, and decisions about who may join the partnership and who will be asked to leave. It is also responsible for designing a performance evaluation process and professional development standards.

With teacher ownership, the partnership becomes directly accountable for learning results and educational outcomes. If learning does not take place to the satisfaction of the clients, parents, and students, the practice cannot remain in business. Student learning becomes paramount. As a result, teachers in a professional partnership think in new ways about the introduction and use of technology. Because teachers control the budget and the learning program, and because they are responsible for outcomes, technology becomes a tool to help achieve the bottom line of student learning. Just as the medical profession continually introduces new research and technologies to keep its practices current, teachers who are members of a TPP evaluate the latest techniques for improving learning.

Early evidence from EdVisions Cooperative, a professional partnership formed as a cooperative, suggests that the whole dynamic of teaching and learning changes as noted above. The teachers in schools run by the cooperative have chosen to pay themselves higher than average salaries, and the technology budget of the school has also been set higher than average. The learning programs are developed, implemented, and improved by the teachers. Teachers, students, and parents form close relationships geared toward learning. Each teacher is expected to develop and implement his or her own professional development plan. Evaluation is by peer review, and teachers who have failed to perform have been asked to leave.

# WHY WOULD TEACHERS WANT TO OWN A PROFESSIONAL PRACTICE?

The teaching profession is facing great challenges today in terms of attracting and retaining a sufficient number of high quality teachers and in finding the time and means for professional development. An estimated 50 percent of new teachers resign from teaching within their first five years. This startling statistic suggests that existing organizational arrangements for teachers simply are not providing them with the opportunity to practice their profession in meaningful or rewarding ways.

The teacher ownership model changes the dynamic of these concerns by providing teachers with the opportunity to take charge of their professional lives. As members of a TPP, teachers have a greater opportunity to shape and implement a shared educational vision and culture. They gain greater control over daily operations that affect their professional lives and have greater influence over administrative decisions that affect learning outcomes. As partners of a TPP, teachers can create opportunities for more interdependence with other professionals, and they can design more effective means to improve student and parent involvement. Because they are in charge, teachers can experience an expanded sense of creativity, challenge, and reward.

Yet with these benefits come more responsibility and more risk. Greater autonomy is a trade-off for less security, both at a personal level and an organizational level. There is no tenure—no guarantee of a job. Teachers will be required to take greater personal responsibility for student achievement. While the development of a TPP presents teachers with the opportunity to realize some of their long-sought goals, they lose the protection offered by union contracts. At an organizational level, those who do not perform stand to lose their contracts with clients, and, ultimately, their business. It is also important to understand that in a TPP teachers take on responsibilities they do not have as employees, namely, responsibility for administrative decisions such as personnel and budget. Some teachers may prefer not to have such responsibilities.

Forming and running a business entails risks and responsibilities that may not be suited to everybody. As with the decision to start any small business, the decision to form a TPP should be weighed carefully, after thoughtful study of what is involved. The remainder of this guide helps illuminate what is involved in running a TPP and highlights some of the major implications that teachers, as well as other organizations, may want to consider as they evaluate the potential, and the potential impact, of TPPs.

# WHO ARE THE POTENTIAL CLIENTS OF TEACHER PROFESSIONAL PARTNERSHIPS?

Teacher professional partnerships exist to educate students. However, the TPP is not guaranteed any students. TPPs must identify persons or entities, referred to in this guide as "clients," to provide them with access to students and funding to pay for these students' education.

Clients purchase educational services from a TPP—clients are agents for students. Access to students and revenues results from a relationship with the client, generally by way of a contract.

The most obvious plan for a teacher partnership is to run a whole, single school. There is some literature on teacher-run schools, and some such schools exist. This is one manifestation of the general idea to which the ownership dimension can be added.

However, teacher-run schools are not the only model. A TPP could offer specialized services, run a part of a school, or run a program cutting across several schools, for example, a mathematics or art department or special education. TPPs could also sell their services outside of schools. For example, the tax credit law in Minnesota creates a public market for supplementary education: summer language camps, advanced or remedial tutoring and so forth. Parents make the decisions and are reimbursed from the tax credit. The truly private markets are also open, such as families who pay for instruction with their own money or business firms that buy education for their employees. What follows is a discussion of potential clients for TPPs in elementary and secondary education, considering both school and non-school education.

## OPPORTUNITIES IN SCHOOLS

### The Charter Sector

The opportunity to start and run a school has opened up since 1991—for TPPs as well as for others—as a result of decisions in thirty-eight or more states to create a "charter sector" within public education. These schools are nonprofit corporations or the equivalent, with the authority under law to contract for services, including instruction. The teacher partnership simply becomes the contractor.

A charter school is not a kind of school; it is not a learning model or a pedagogy. A charter is an empty structure—as a building is an empty structure—into which someone puts some kind of learning program, hopefully a different and better one. The charter sector is intended to be, in large part, a research and development program for public education. The goal is for people to try things. To this end, the states have cut charter schools free from many of the regulations that prescribe content and process in district schools. Charter schools are meant to be accountable for results, for student and fiscal performance.

Charter schools can be formed new or, under the laws of most of the charter states, they may be formed by converting an existing school to charter status. Conversion sometimes requires either the initiative or the approval of teachers working in the school.

A model of a TPP that appeared in 1994 at EdVisions Cooperative serves several whole charter schools. As of 2001, EdVisions Cooperative serves eight whole schools, five secondary and three elementary, sponsored by seven different entities including four school districts, two universities, and the Minnesota Department of Children, Families, and Learning.

## The District Sector

There has been little, if any, contracting for instruction within the district sector of public education. It has been assumed that teachers are and will always be "employees."

But because charter schools may be sponsored by boards of education, the charter sector does offer a portal into the district sector for teacher partnerships. Teachers could propose a new charter school for board approval, or they could send the board a proposal for conversion of an existing school. Or the board might take the initiative to form a school and ask teachers if they would like to form a professional partnership to run it. A TPP can become part of the mainline program of district public education in any one of these ways.

Contracting directly with the district outside the charter law is more difficult. This option may have to wait for further changes in state law and policy. Still, a contract for instruction (to manage the learning program) may be possible with the permission of the bargaining agent; and the bargaining agent may be willing to agree if its own teacher members are the ones asking for the arrangement.

Under traditional arrangements—the traditional, centralized model of district decision making—the TPP would contract with the school board of the district. But if districts do begin to delegate decision-making authority to the schools, as has been recommended by the Education Commission of the States and by John Murphy and Dennis Doyle in *Redesigning the Operating Environments in School Districts and Schools* (Murphy and Doyle, 2001), the TPP could find itself negotiating for the contract with the leadership—the principal or site council—of the school.

A TPP might be set up to run a learning program for a district through the board of education at any of three levels:

- A whole school: As discussed above, a new charter school could be started or an existing school converted to a charter, then handled by the teacher partnership.
- A department of a school: Teachers in the mathematics department of a large high school, for example, might propose to form a TPP that would contract for the handling of all the teaching of mathematics in the school. They would receive a negotiated fee

for service and be given the authority to set up the teaching and learning as, in their professional judgment, they thought best. They would be required to demonstrate student achievement. It is easy to envision this arrangement working for teachers handling the arts, world languages, or sciences, as well.

- A district wide program: A TPP might contract with a district to run a program operating at multiple sites within a district. At the high school level the teachers in this TPP might handle the math or the science or language departments of all the secondary schools in a multi–high school district. The multischool character might be a part of the plan from the outset, or it might evolve over time. Minneapolis, for example, has the Montessori program as one of its learner options at the elementary level. Teachers in these Montessori schools could form a partnership to run their program at all the sites, with the lead teachers at each site making up a council to govern the program districtwide.

One particular program in the district sector is worth special attention—the so-called alternative schools. These schools began to appear in Minnesota and across the country after 1970. They were designed for students "not doing well" in regular schools. Alternative schools and programs now account for a surprisingly large proportion of secondary school enrollment. A few of these schools (in Minneapolis especially) are nonprofit corporations contracted to their district, but most have been established by the district.

In 2001 in Minnesota, more than 100,000 students, out of a total school population in grades 7–12 of approximately 450,000, attend alternative schools for some portion of the year. Essentially, these are students for whom the district still claims state aid, although they are turned over to the alternative schools. They are mainly students who have not been successful in regular schools. Alternative schools have a good deal of flexibility and discretion in the kind of programs they run, so they are logical clients for new and different learning programs, which TPPs might offer.

## As a Subcontractor

Another setting for a TPP is as a subcontractor to or a partner with one of the emerging education businesses in the industry—education management organizations (EMOs). In the early years most of the companies in this education industry had a fairly defined learning program and business model, and most of them, like almost everybody else, thought in terms of employing teachers. Over time, with experience, some have become more flexible. Edison Schools, a private manager of public schools, for example, is willing to work under the charter law or on direct contract to the district. It is willing to hire teachers itself or to take over and manage teachers employed by the district.

There may be a good deal of flexibility in this emerging relationship, and entrepreneurial teachers might find opportunities here. An EMO might be willing to contract with a district or charter school to provide a particular learning design and then subcontract with a TPP to carry out the teaching. An EMO might also be willing to let the TPP have the primary contract with the district or charter school and then let the teachers buy its learning design. In this instance, the "learning business" would work for the teachers—the TPP would buy and implement the learning model (and related materials and technology) provided by the EMO.

### The Nonpublic Sector

What applies here to the district sector also applies to the private sector of K–12 education. These independent and parochial schools account for about 11 percent of total enrollment in the United States. As in the district sector, the TPP might consider owning and running a whole school or a department of a school or might serve a number of schools as clients.

## OPPORTUNITIES BEYOND SCHOOLS

### Families

Households are significant buyers of education for their children. Many of the courses and lessons parents purchase for their children are essentially extracurricular activities, such as music or sports. But, increasingly, they have to with academics:

- Home school: Some academic instruction in home school settings is for mainline schooling. This now accounts for approximately

3 percent of enrollment. However, it is becoming less and less common for parents to act as teachers in home school settings. Parents rely more and more on the Internet and learning materials sold to them by others. With increasing frequency, the materials and methods are supplied to them by (former) teachers.

- Tutoring: Tutoring is generally thought of as supplementary to work in school. It may either be to help students catch up on material they have missed in school or to help successful students move ahead faster. Using modern electronics, teachers can now work as tutors offsite, serving students regularly enrolled in school or students schooled at home. This form of tutoring can be done on a local basis, but it can also be done now on a fully national basis. For an example, see www.tutor.com (Kohn and Baird, 1999–2001).

To appreciate fully the potential of this home sector, it is useful to consider the implications of states now introducing performance measures for school completion. Increasingly, states mandate that the diploma be awarded only when students demonstrate they have mastered what is required by the standards. The flip side of this mandate is the opportunity it affords students to get the diploma *whenever they can demonstrate they know what the standards require.* In other words, students can graduate—get a diploma—without having to earn all the credits in school. To the extent that it is in students' best interest to move through high school faster and to begin their careers sooner, there is a potential market for teachers who know how to help them do this.

## Preschool

As the child day care industry grows, it has also taken on more of an educational component. In 1986, Alan Campbell, then a senior executive of Aramark said, "We're opening a school a week in this country." He was referring to what most people then would still have called day care centers (Kolderie, June 1984).

Given the research pointing to the importance of school readiness to subsequent learning, efforts are continuing to expand the public role in preschool. Interesting questions and possibilities will arise in the case of childcare programs proposed to operate at public school sites, before and after the regular school day. Will the program be organized by the district because it is located in the school? Or will it be organized by the counties, which, in some states, such as Minnesota, oversee public childcare programs? County governments are much more experienced with contract arrangements than are school districts. Typically counties do not—and do not want to—own and run the day care programs; they purchase services. This situation could open an opportunity for teachers in groups to provide, at a minimum, the educational element of child-care programs. (In some states where the districts contract with private childcare firms, the firms may hire the teachers.)

## Adults

In addition to preschool and K–12 settings, there is also the entire field of adult education to consider. Adults buy learning and training for themselves for a variety of reasons and from a variety of sources. The community education or continuing education programs of any large school district include a wide range and variety of offerings. These arms of the district are also relatively more open to contract arrangements for instruction than many traditional K–12 settings.

## Business Firms

Employers also buy learning and training for their employees. Much of this is college-level work. In the aggregate, "corporate higher education" is quite substantial. Nell Eurich (1990) estimated that the learning enterprise within American business is as large as all of conventional higher education combined. As such, it is a potential field for teacher professional partnerships. In the 1980s, a bright college graduate, Jessica Shaten, returned from the Peace Corps to run a math tutoring business, Math Unlimited Minnesota. Among her clients, for example, was 3M Company, which retained her to teach statistics and experimental design to middle management executives.

Opportunities exist outside of college-level work, as well. In the summer of 2001, the suburban city of Oakdale, Minnesota, retained a teacher from Tartan High School to give police officers and other city staff a basic introduction to Spanish. Markets similar to this one may grow.

**3**

# WHAT ARE THE KEY INGREDIENTS OF SUCCESS?

Teachers starting a new partnership will want to know how to do it well and will need to understand the key ingredients of a successful partnership: culture and leadership; the learning program; and paying attention to business essentials.

## CULTURE AND LEADERSHIP

The design and development of a TPP is founded on a vision in which teachers, parents, and the community collaborate for the mutual benefit of students. The primary goal of the learning environment is to provide a teacher-led dynamic, resulting in an effective high-achieving learning community. The curriculum consists not only of what is written, but also of what is actually taught and learned. Everyone in the organization knows the ultimate purpose is to develop responsible and fully capable human beings.

To achieve that goal, the culture and the leadership of the organization must provide an atmosphere of creativity, achievement, and accountability. Members of the organization must also provide talents and take responsibility for the TPP's success.

The creation of the appropriate culture and leadership is a critical success factor for TPPs. Often professional groups assume that appropriate culture and leadership will occur because they are comprised of persons of good will who are competent members of a profession centered on a higher purpose. This kind of thinking can be a fatal mistake. Creating and sustaining the culture and leadership desired by the group is very hard work. However, striving to develop the appropriate culture and leadership will create the most effective and satisfying organization for all involved. Without clearly defined expectations and values, a culture may evolve that is not aligned with the goals of the organization.

## The Working Definition of Culture

The culture of a TPP will be defined by the commonly held values of its members: the behaviors that are the accepted norms, as well as the members' interactions, attitudes, and shared traditions and practices. A TPP cultivates a culture as it continually and purposefully strives to be a learning place that is caring, creative, communicative, self-reflective, celebratory, and purposeful. For the TPP to be successful, the members' personal values must be aligned with the organizational values (Collary, Dunlap, Enloe, and Gagnon, 1998).

The expectations of the culture are based on a commonly held mission and vision for the TPP. Leaders and members must relentlessly uphold the highest expectations for the organization and for teacher and student performance, fostering a culture of constant growth and improvement.

## Characteristics of Successful Professional Partnerships

Some professional partnerships are more successful than others. Successful partnerships exhibit the following:

- Power rests with the members who learn to operate independently and interdependently. Members who join the organization want shared resources and skill enhancement.

- Work, such as curriculum development and outcomes measurement, is coordinated through knowledge shared by the professionals.
- Control relies extensively on systems designed for meeting the needs of children and the goals of the organization.
- Parents and children have a role in coordinating activities in the organization.
- Functional units in the organization support the professional needs of the teachers (for example, committee structures for consensus decisions about the professional partnership).
- Leaders are successful only when they are perceived as serving the teachers and the children. Leadership is not only the duty of formal leaders. Leadership is expected from all members of the TPP at various times for various needs.
- Selection of the members is most important to the success of the organization (Fogel, 1990). The most successful organizations select members with histories of success.

## Expected Behaviors in a Successful TPP

The values of the TPP help define the expected behaviors of all persons associated with the TPP. The expected behaviors for a successful TPP are:

- Collaboration—working together to achieve a common end without regard for status or position. Collaboration requires the willingness and ability to build and sustain strong professional relationships with other members.
- Civility—treating each other with respect, dignity, and kindness. (This does not mean an absence of creative conflict, challenge, or accountability.)
- Communication—clearly stating candid ideas and thoughts about achieving the goals.
- Cocreation—allowing for everyone in the organization to play a role in achieving the goals:
  - Children are apprentices, learners and participants in setting goals and determining their own learning program.

- The child's parents are collaborators with the teachers in setting the goals for the child. Parents also have some choice in how the organization can best serve the needs of the child.
- Teachers are coleaders. They exercise professional judgment in the determination of appropriate methods and pedagogy for achieving the goals. Teachers also need influencing skills to persuade parents of the appropriateness of the teacher's recommendations.
- Accountability—taking personal responsibility for one's performance and acknowledging one's responsibility for achieving the goals. Every member assumes personal responsibility for the performance of the whole organization.
  - Teachers—agree to be accountable to mutually agreed-upon measures of effectiveness.
  - Parents—agree to support and encourage the educational efforts of their children.
- Commitment to continuous improvement—planning, executing, evaluating, and modifying processes and systems.
- Commitment to development—using research and current assessment data to develop and improve.

## TPP Members' Accountability

The professionals in the TPP are self-regulating. Each professional is accountable to the student, the family, and his or her peers:

- Teacher members conduct peer reviews and hold each other accountable for professional performance.
- Teacher members review and evaluate each other's work for quality and outcomes.
- Members lead efforts in continuous improvement.
- Teacher members discipline other teachers for failure to perform within the accepted cultural values of collaboration, reciprocity, and mutual respect.
- Teacher members report the results of their professional reviews and evaluations to the parents and sponsoring body.

- Members help each other improve by peer coaching and mentoring, reflective practice, learning circles, and other methods.
- Members use research data, external review data, and other data sources for continuous improvement.

## Other Characteristics of Membership

All members of the TPP have additional responsibilities and behaviors that are essential for the overall success of the organization. The successful member of the TPP:

- Demonstrates professional command of a body of knowledge about teaching and learning that reflects self-motivated creativity.
- Embraces change.
- Continually enhances skills.
- Demonstrates openness to objective evaluation by respected peers, with the objectives of knowing when he or she has succeeded and identifying opportunities for improvement.
- Possesses communication and relationship development skills.
- Shares information with parents and peers.
- Exhibits openness to opportunities for improvement.
- Strives for successful team membership.
- Develops a wide network of contacts within and outside the organization and seeks new learning (Quinn, Anderson, and Finkelstein, 1996).

## Evaluation, Decision-Making Processes, and Planning

In addition to the above, there are several other factors that define a successful TPP:

- Evaluation is a key, frequent, and ongoing process in the organization. Evaluative practices should be built into the culture of the organization (e.g., part of weekly team meetings). Measurements are carefully selected and openly reported, and actions with the potential to have a direct impact are taken based on those measurements.

- By necessity, decision processes must be situational. Therefore, emergent decisions may need to be made solely by the leader. However, the goal of the organization is to create an environment where effective consensus decisions are the norm.
- The TPP is a learning organization that respects and honors new knowledge.
- Members share lessons learned from successes, mistakes, experiments, and continuous improvement.
- The organization consciously seeks the best teachers for membership.
- The organization plans well, with an overall strategy to reach its goals and annual work plans that move the organization toward those final goals (Marr and Zismer, 1998).
- The organization is fiscally responsible, accountable, and sound. It supports professional management and fiscal integrity.

## Other Dimensions of Leadership

The successful TPP has a leadership group that supports creativity and commitment to its goals. Every member of a TPP will be called upon to be a leader in a variety of situations. To build high-functioning teams, each member must respect professional autonomy.

In addition, there may also be individuals who are assigned leadership positions within the TPP. In some cases, an individual will be chosen. The successful leader of the TPP would be selected by his or her peers from a slate of qualified peers. The leader is not the boss but first among equals, the *principal teacher*, who is also evaluated by his or her peers.

Successful leaders have the following characteristics (Kusy, Essex, and Marr, 1995):

- Clarity of purpose—the motivation of the leader is to achieve the goals of the organization, not personal power or prestige.
- Ability to sustain the focus of others on a vision and aim—the leader effectively paints the vision of the future for all and helps others understand how their work leads to that end. The leader paves the way for others' success by removing obstacles, sharing information freely, calling upon everyone's unique talents, and sharing decisions.

- Ability to inspire trust and credibility—the leader is trusted and credible. Trust is earned by doing what one promises and by personal honesty and integrity. Credibility is built by a history and /or concurrent experience as a successful teacher as judged by peers, parents, and children.
- Political savvy—the leader builds a strong base of influence within the organization and the larger community. He or she understands the needs of each subgroup and meets those needs in alignment with the organization's goals and objectives. The leader has high-level skills in negotiation and persuasion.
- A service attitude—the leader embodies a servant–leadership model. The leader's role is to serve others. In other words, the effective TPP leader is not autocratic or controlling but is a team builder, drawing others into leadership roles. The leader cherishes a diversity of opinions and cultures and demonstrates this value by showing respect for each individual.
- Appreciation for others' success—the leader shares responsibility and proclaims others' successes publicly. The leader recognizes everyone's unique contributions to the organization.
- Keen self-awareness—the leader needs to know his or her personal strengths and weaknesses, accept them, and select others to complement his or her talents. The leader understands that language frames the culture and uses language that will build the cultural values.
- Responsibility and accountability—the leader is responsible for his or her actions and for the outcomes of the organization (Kusy, Essex, and Marr, 1995).

## THE LEARNING PROGRAM

The power of the TPP model is nowhere more apparent than in the selection or design and implementation of the learning model. TPP partners have the opportunity to fully express their professional aspirations through the selection or creation of a complete learning program, along with the resources to implement the program (budget, staffing, compensation, technology, books, etc.). It is through these opportunities that TPPs offer the greatest hope for substantial gain in student learning.

While TPPs should be guided by research in the selection or design of learning programs, experimentation and creativity are also essential as they lead to break-through gains in learning. The opportunity to create the learning model and learning programs is what will attract most teachers to the TPP model. Opportunities exist here both for teachers with responsibility for running an entire school, as well as for those who offer a single subject (Reason and Bradbury, 2001).

The very nature of the TPP, as it has been defined here, will change the nature of the learning community. The fact that the TPP will be held accountable for improving student performance and meeting the needs and expectations of students, parents, and the contracting entity will result in a much greater focus on individual student achievement.

Clearly, teachers in every educational environment try to reach individual students. In the TPP environment this effort can be intensified and carried to a new level. It will be essential for teachers to understand the individual differences in learning and skills of each student and to work with each student individually. Individualized or student-centered learning will not only be the natural result of the culture but also of the economic imperative to improve performance.

Teachers interested in forming a TPP will have many ideas about the most appropriate learning program. In most cases, the challenge will not be lack of ideas. The challenge will be to get all partners of the TPP to agree and fully commit to a common approach, as well as to agree to a method by which to measure progress and the means by which to improve, based on their experience. One of the difficulties at any school is that the initial planning makes assumptions about the individual students whom the planners expect to enroll. The reality is that once the TPP knows who the actual students are, the plan will need to be altered to meet the needs of those individuals.

This guide will not suggest a specific learning program. However, there are some considerations that members of a TPP should take into account in selecting or designing their own program. A learning program should be standards-based (in this context standards are stated expectations for learning, not state-regulated standards), use a multitude of assessments, include differentiated activities for learners, and employ research-based learning strategies.

## Standards-Based Learning

All learning programs, regardless of their scope, should be standards-based. A standard may be described as a broad description of knowledge and skills that students are expected to acquire in this learning experience. A standard stated with a behavior for achieving it provides better understanding and direction to the teacher, to the learner, and to the parent of the expectations required by the program. A quality, standards-based learning program should also include benchmarks that are sub-components of the standard. These should identify age-appropriate skill levels and define expectations as the student progresses through the learning experience.

In a quality, standards-based learning program design, students should be given vast experiences and opportunities to demonstrate their progress toward these benchmarks. The standards will be clearer and more meaningful to the TPP partners if they are written by TPP partners themselves.

Every content area has a national standards document. Many states have their own standards. Minnesota, for example, has frameworks in various content areas. And teachers also have their own ideas about standards. TPP members should review these documents, policies, and ideas as they design and write the standards they will use in their learning program.

## Assessment

A second component of a quality learning program is assessment. In *Assessing Student Learning: New Rules, New Realities,* Brandt (1998) describes five major reasons for assessment: (1) *Accountability* to school boards, community members, and policy makers; (2) *Program evaluation* to appraise the improvements in various programs (e.g., a new spelling program); (3) *Classroom feedback* to provide information to teachers about the performance of their classes; (4) *Student performance* to indicate specific achievement by individual students (this information is usually shared with the student and parent); and (5) *Graduation and matriculation* to evaluate individual student skills and knowledge acquisition against preset benchmarks, a practice that is becoming more prevalent in standards-based systems (Brandt, 1998).

The key to assessments is that they must allow the student, the parent, and the teacher to clearly see that the student is demonstrating progress toward achieving the standards. Evaluations should incorporate state-mandated testing, norm-referenced testing, student and parent surveys, and frequent narratives to the parents and contracting entity regarding the students' progress through the benchmarks and standards. TPPs should offer parents, students, and contracting entities opportunities for input into the system that are both formal, such as surveys, organized activities, and home visits, and informal, such as e-mail, suggestion boxes, and an atmosphere that is welcoming and open to them. The scope of involvement may depend, in part, on the service provided. For example, a total education program for a student needs much more input, especially from parents, than a program providing physics instruction for a series of school districts.

## Differentiated Learning Experiences and Activities

The third component of a learning program is the actual learning experiences and activities in which the student will be engaged. The learning experiences should be designed to help the individual student progress toward the standards. The TPP should decide what constitutes the major learning experiences and activities to assure the continuity of the learning program and to assure appropriate skill acquisition by all learners. The program should contain sufficient freedom to allow students who have unique interests to expand on these interests during their journey toward meeting the standards.

## Research-Based Learning Strategies and Methods

Each teacher brings his or her own approach, methods and strategies to the TPP for helping students learn successfully. These methods reflect the teacher's professional experience and judgment and may relate to his or her personality. Methods that work for one teacher may not work for another. In this guide, we will not define or analyze the various tools used by professional educators to assure learning. TPP members, however, should have research-based strategies in their learning program's arsenal and must make sure that all of the professionals in the group know how and when to use them.

## PAYING ATTENTION TO BUSINESS ESSENTIALS

It must be clear to all members of a TPP that the purpose or the product (to use a market term) of a TPP is to develop and provide an educational program that achieves the desired level of student performance. Partners of the TPP must never lose sight of this fundamental reality. The TPP will fail and cease to exist unless it succeeds in meeting the needs and expectations of the clients, the students, and the parents.

The other fundamental reality is that the TPP will fail and cease to exist if it does not manage its fiscal and other business affairs appropriately. Therefore, in addition to their professional role of developing the entire educational program and achieving the desired levels of student performance, the partners of a TPP must also manage and administer the business.

All professional partnerships are businesses. The business affairs of the partnership must be properly addressed and the members of the partnership held strictly accountable for the results. In a TPP, teachers are owners—not just owners of the educational program but also owners of the entire enterprise, and they must act as owners of a small business.

For many professionals in education, as well as in other fields such as medicine, perceiving their profession as a business is not comfortable. For some, it takes away the intrinsic motivation and satisfaction from the profession. These individuals want to be driven by a service motive, not by a profit motive. Teachers who are thinking of forming or joining a TPP need to understand that the most successful businesses are driven by a desire to provide excellent service, to meet and exceed the expectations of the persons being served, and to generate a risk-rated return on the money invested in the business. The difference between a public entity and a business is that a business is subject to the harsh realities of the market—if a business doesn't "deliver," it can't continue to exist.

In previous sections of this guide we have addressed some of the essentials of running a successful TPP (i.e., the culture and the learning program). What follows is a discussion of the essentials of managing and administering a business.

### Business Management and Administration

The TPP needs business expertise and experience, as well as the technical systems to support the organization. Being a part of a partnership does not require all teachers to be involved in management or administration. It does require that all partners make certain there is good management and administration and that they pay close attention to the details of how well it is done.

The TPP needs to hire someone with appropriate business expertise and experience to manage the business affairs of the partnership. In this case, "hiring" may mean that individual partners of the TPP who have the requisite experience will be asked to work for, and be paid by, the partners of the TPP in this capacity. It may mean that the TPP avails itself of the services of an outside organization that provides business management to many TPPs. It may mean that several TPPs have a joint business manager who serves each TPP some portion of the week as is commonly done in physician practices. The business manager works for the partners of the TPP. This person needs to have (or have access to someone with) in-depth knowledge of financial management and school finance.

The TPP needs someone with business skills, and it also needs the technical systems to support the organization. Chief among these systems are payroll and accounting. These, too, may be provided by the TPP itself or done in conjunction with others.

## A Plan and a Budget

The TPP must know what it wants to do, how it plans to do it, how it will measure/monitor success, where the revenue will come from, how it will be spent, the cash flow requirements, and the capital requirements. The TPP needs a business plan. The business plan exists for the benefit of the partners. It provides direction, focus, measurement, and accountability. It is also a key document in dealing with lenders and/or grantmakers to secure financing.

A business plan is a succinctly articulated definition of the TPP's activities, including multiyear financials. It lays out the vision, mission, values, and details of how the TPP will operate as a professional partnership. A complete business plan should be developed as a part of the process for establishing any new business. Typically the plan is for three years and is updated annually so that the organization always has a three-year plan.

Most new TPPs will find it worthwhile to consult with a business professional familiar with the development of start-up business plans who can facilitate the development of the plan. It is very important to understand the unique circumstances of the specific new start-up TPP. It is also important for the new owners to be aware of what they themselves do and do not understand about starting and running a small business.

In appendix C, "Outline of a Business Plan for a Teacher Professional Partnership," we provide an outline of a potential business plan for a start-up TPP. A good overview of a business plan can also be found in *Charter School Facilities: A Resource Guide on Development and Financing* (2000), which was prepared under the sponsorship of the National Cooperative Bank Development Corporation and the Charter Friends National Network. While this document is directed toward those considering financing a charter school facility, it is a good primer on the general elements of a business plan for any business. Another good resource is a publication of the Department of Treasury, Internal Revenue Service, and Small Business Administration titled *Small Business Resource Guide* (2001).

## Measuring and Monitoring Progress

The TPP must know where it stands relative to its goals and budget. The partners have fiduciary and programmatic responsibility for everything the TPP does. It is the partners' responsibility to ensure that progress is measured and monitored and corrections are made as necessary. All of the partners play a strong role in the monitoring process, not just the individuals who are assigned the task of preparing the information.

Because of their professional interests, members of the TPP will tend, naturally, to pay attention to measuring and monitoring the educational program. As partners of a TPP it is essential that they also pay attention to the fiduciary side of the business.

## No Margin, No Mission

The TPP must manage its affairs well enough to generate a positive bottom line. At the end of the year, the partners may choose to distribute the profits among all partners or all members. They may also decide to use the money for investment in the business (e.g., expansion, staff development, better technology, cash flow requirements). The financial resources must be managed as carefully as the educational program.

## Adequate Financing and Capital Requirements

Capital requirements must be addressed realistically and adequate capital must be available. One of the biggest mistakes start-up organizations make is to underestimate the capital required to start and operate the business.

Typically, a start-up TPP will need financial resources for both the process of developing the business plan (including legal documents) and for some consulting on the development of the business plan (including financial projections). As the TPP begins to operate it will need working capital to provide its cash flow. The TPP will be able to project revenue based on the number of students it expects, along with the timing of the receipt of the money. It must determine when its payroll and other expenses will be paid and make certain that it has sufficient cash on hand to meet it obligations. Capital may be acquired as loans, investment by the partners, and grants.

## Annual Outside Audit

TPPs need a completely objective outside audit once a year—an audit by someone not otherwise connected to the TPP with the requisite skills in accounting, taxation, finance, and management. It is essential that the audit be totally objective and that it review all of the financial transactions, the balance sheet, and financial management.

## 4

# WHAT ARE THE OPTIONS FOR THE DESIGN AND OPERATION OF A TEACHER PROFESSIONAL PARTNERSHIP?

There are many practical questions to consider when designing and operating a TPP: What type of legal entity will suit the group's needs? How should the group's affairs be governed and administered? What size partnership is best, and how will the business functions be accomplished? What type of professional standards of practice should be used? Who will be a partner and how will new members be admitted? How will pay be administered, and how will pension and fringe benefits be handled? What follows describes the options available for the design and operation of TPPs. A group's choices with regard to design and operation will depend on its particular needs and circumstances.

## OPTIONS FOR THE LEGAL STRUCTURE

As in other professions, there are a number of legal structures that may be available to teachers who wish to form a TPP. TPPs may choose to be a cooperative, a partnership, a limited liability company, or a corporation (nonprofit or for-profit). Each of these legal structures provides certain advantages and disadvantages relative to the other alternatives. The ultimate decision about the legal structure for a TPP can be complex and will depend on the group's specific objectives. Teachers contemplating the formation of a professional partnership should obtain competent legal advice to assist in evaluating the organizational structure that will best help them meet their objectives.

In appendix A, "Comparison of Legal Structures for Doing Business as a Teacher Professional Organization," we identify the organizational options and present information on ownership, duration, liability exposure, transferability of interests, governance responsibility, and tax characteristics of each option. In addition to the customary legal and tax considerations outlined in appendix A, there are a number of other factors to consider in the context of TPPs. In selecting a structure for a TPP, consideration should be given to the implication of the structure for political and public relations purposes. To the extent that public funding is ultimately paying the teachers, public officials must be comfortable with the structure.

## GOVERNANCE AND ADMINISTRATION

Thinking through the governance, management, and administration of the TPP is essential. This new entity is a business and should be run as a business. In some public or service organizations issues of governance, executive leadership and management/administration are not clearly defined. Such blurring of roles in a business would lead to failure. For a TPP to succeed, both the education delivery side and the business side of the TPP must be clearly defined.

Who owns, who controls, and who benefits are three key questions that need to be answered as teachers make decisions about the kind of business they wish to form. What they hope to accomplish as a TPP should drive the development of governance, executive leadership, and management/administration. Decisions need to be made about the distribution of financial returns and other benefits that may be realized by many others besides the partners, such as associates, students, administrators, and parents.

As explained above, there are several different legal structures to choose from in developing a TPP. No matter what type of legal structure is chosen, the rules of governance are similar. Articles of incorporation constitute the TPP's contract with the state as far as the type of organization to be formed and a general description of what the organization will do. Bylaws spell out the contract with the teacher members and give details on the governance of the organization. Who makes decisions and the process for making those decisions are matters of vital importance to the success of the organization.

The size of the business has an impact on the governance, executive leadership, and management/administration. Size does not rule out types of approaches, but sometimes there is less room for error and flexibility in larger businesses.

The business is made up of four groups. The roles and responsibilities of each group should be spelled out in the planning process. The partners own the business; the board of directors sets the policy and direction; the executive leadership leads the work of the business; and the management/administration handles the day-to-day tasks.

## Partners

Partners must *own* the business. This means much more than the legal document that says that the partners own something. Every partner must accept personal responsibility for his or her own performance, as well as for the performance of the students and the organization as a whole. Owning a business represents a major change from working for someone else, especially if that work has been in a traditional school setting. It will require excellent communication skills, teamwork, and a new set of skills necessary for determining if the organization is accomplishing what it set out to do and if it remains financially viable.

If there is to be full ownership by the partners in the business, all partners need to be able to participate. This does not mean, necessarily, that all members need to be involved in setting direction or management. However, they do need to have access to enough information to achieve a certain comfort level with the governance, management, and administration. At a minimum, this means holding an annual meeting, providing a financial audit, and periodic communication. Some new businesses attempt "continuous communication" with partners in order to build full ownership and participation.

## Board of Directors

Boards set policy and direction and make sure the business is on track with the vision and mission. Boards typically, but not always, hire and evaluate the executive/leader, approve budgets, set compensation, propose changes in articles and bylaws to the membership, and have fiduciary responsibility for the business. Boards can be comprised of elected partners or can include all the partners. In smaller professional organizations, boards are often made up of all the partners.

Generally, there are four officers of the board: chair, vice-chair, treasurer, and secretary. If the board is large, a committee structure is often used to make nonstrategic decisions or to allow in-depth discussion of specific issues. Common committees are finance, audit, personnel and compensation, and planning. An executive committee can be used in place of the other committees or as an additional committee. Committees can be comprised of a mix of board members and non–board members. In some cases the TPP may choose to have some persons who are not partners or members of the TPP serve on committees.

Boards need to spend their time and energy on policy and monitoring the performance of the business, not on management and administrative details. Although any size board can be effective, a smaller board (with an odd number of members) has a better chance of success than larger boards. Boards need to be able to make decisions in a timely manner, and the process needs to be seen by the members and other board members as fair. Some people believe that the board of directors reflects the soul of a business. By law, boards have a fiduciary responsibility, and successful boards know and live the vision and the mission of the business.

## Executive Leadership

The board of directors will set the direction—how and by whom will the work of the business get accomplished? How will the business be organized and directed? There are number of options for the structure (e.g., hierarchical, informal), and many options for executive leadership titles and roles (e.g., executive director, CEO, president, lead teacher, managing partner).

These are significant decisions. They will have a strong impact on the chances of success for the enterprise. In a small business it may be preferable to have a flat, rather than a hierarchical structure, with a managing partner, rather than a CEO. This decision will be driven by the vision and mission of the business and by what process will be used to accomplish the mission. (See section in chapter 3 titled, "Culture and Leadership.")

### Management/Administration

There are numerous day-to-day tasks required to run the business and the school. Who will be doing these tasks? On the business side, these tasks include such things as payroll, accounting, state reports, insurance, pension plan administration, purchasing, personnel systems, and marketing. On the school side tasks include scheduling, peer review, quality review, professional development, serving as back-up staff, and credentialing. The TPP may decide that members will do all of these tasks. However, in many professional businesses, doctors, lawyers, and accountants have found that the skills that make them good in their professional life are not the same skills needed to run a business. They often have a managing partner who works with a business manager. Another variation of this arrangement would be to have comanagers, one with responsibility for the business side and the other for the school side. Some tasks may be "outsourced," contracting with outside vendors of services, including one the TPP forms with other similar TPPs. For example, if the TPP is formed as a cooperative, it may form another cooperative made up of TPPs—a regional or secondary service cooperative. Another option is to contract for services with an outside organization, such as a service organization, as described below.

## PARTNERSHIP SIZE AND SERVICE ORGANIZATIONS

The size of the partnership, that is the number of partners in the TPP, is a matter to be carefully considered and should be part of ongoing discussions about the TPP's business plan. If an organization is very small, the professional and business tasks may seem overwhelming to the partners. If the TPP is very large, the individual partner's sense of unity, participation, autonomy, and accountability may be diminished. The problems of a small TPP may be overcome through purchasing some services from a "service organization." The problems of a large organization may be overcome through an intense effort at community/culture building and the relinquishing of some autonomy on the part of individuals and units within the organization.

In determining the right size for itself, each TPP should give consideration to many factors, including: (1) the number, of persons the members of the TPP believe can be in the organization and still allow it to successfully achieve the desired culture; (2) the size, number, and complexity of the learning community created; (3) the ability to provide high quality and cost-effective administrative and professional services. The partners must make trade-offs in determining their optimal size.

## TPP Size and Culture

As stated earlier, one of the key ingredients of success for a TPP is the creation of a learning community that provides an atmosphere of creativity, achievement, and accountability. Other characteristics include a community in which the members: know and understand each other; are interdependent; feel ownership; act in the knowledge that they have accountability for the performance of the entire TPP; have a fair and inclusive decision-making process, and share values as well as a common mission and vision. This is an uncommon culture and one that is very difficult to achieve under the best of circumstances. All organizations engaged in the attempt will have a continuous struggle. This is especially true of organizations in which the members are thoughtful, articulate, used to operating independently, and not accustomed to the interdependence and collegiality necessary to run an entire school or program. The establishment and nurturing of the culture is an ongoing task and one that is crucial.

It goes without saying that the larger the group, the harder it will be to create and maintain the culture. It takes a great deal of time and effort to create the desired culture under the best of circumstances. Similarly, if the culture has already been established, the larger the group, the harder it is for new members to become acclimated.

One of the biggest dangers for an organization is to assume that maintaining a culture will be relatively easy once a small group has created a culture that approximates what the founders envisioned. It is important for members to remind themselves that each new person changes the dynamic of the organization.

One solution is to limit the size of the organization, at least initially, to the number of people who can gather around a table to participate in the deliberations and conversations necessary in a professional partnership. Granted, the table may come in different sizes, depending on the individuals involved and the length of time they have been together.

There are many examples of large accounting, consulting, and law firms. A key consideration of any firm is the professional and financial liabilities of the firm. These liability matters are resolved by having professional, financial, contractual, and legal standards, as well as processes that everyone in the firm must follow. While all TPPs must have these standards in place, it is not practical in large firms to have a process that takes everyone's views into account in applying the standards. This results in a professional trade-off: being part of a large organization in exchange for a loss of some autonomy and participation. By its nature, every organization requires interdependence and limitations on autonomy and participation. Large organizations tend to present more of these limitations than small organizations.

## Size, Number, and Complexity of the Learning Communities Served

Clearly, the size of a TPP is also related to the size required to perform its tasks. The learning communities created will vary in size depending on the clients served and the educational program implemented. Many, but not all, TPPs will be in charge of a complete school operation. Others will address the needs of specific students, specific courses, and other specific educational programs. In each case a learning community needs to be created that fits the individual circumstances.

If the TPP will be responsible for an entire school, the size of the school is clearly relevant: the number of partners required to implement the program will define the minimal size of the TPP. The teachers at

EdVisions Cooperative believe that 100 to 250 students is a desirable size. (See chapter 6.) They believe that schools of this size are better able to create a learning community. Some of the characteristics of this community of learning are: teachers and students get to know each other; students know each other; the focus is on students' individual needs and the learning processes; parent involvement is higher; and members of the community are more accountable to each other.

Another consideration is how many separate learning communities a given TPP can serve effectively. This number is closely linked to considerations of the desired culture, school size, and the number of learning programs.

If there are several sites/learning communities, the following questions are fundamental: Will there be one culture that permeates all sites? Will the learning program, staff salaries, and parental involvement be the same at all sites? Does the entire TPP make decisions for all sites? What autonomy will each site have? How does the TPP deal with its programmatic and financial liability for each site? To summarize, will this be one organization or many organizations under one name/umbrella? The implications of this decision go to the very heart of what the TPP wishes to create. The problems of having one organization with one culture serving multiple sites are real but not insurmountable.

Another important consideration is the complexity of the TPP's learning programs. Can one TPP successfully master, implement, and improve a variety of learning programs, for example, the learning program for grades 7–12 and a different program for grades K–6). Can one TPP master, implement and improve two separate learning programs for grades 7–12? The question is relevant for TPPs serving an entire school or one subject/discipline. The TPP must have partners who can implement its learning programs with a high degree of professional competence.

Ultimately, the partners of the TPP will need to determine the wisdom of having a tight focus versus a broad focus. An organization that implements more than one learning program tends to get separated by these learning programs, and over time it is harder to remain as one partnership because the focus of professional attention and decision making shifts to the individual groupings.

## High-Quality and Cost–Effective Administrative Services

Small physician partnerships, cooperatives, and other professional partnerships have found that survival as a small entity depends upon being able to work with others having similar service needs to achieve the economies of scale enjoyed by large entities. It is a question of access to cost-effective services, expertise in specialized administrative and professional disciplines, and the time requirements on the members of a small partnership.

Smaller entities understand that they must find better and more economic means to purchase services, technology, consulting advice, financial services, pension/benefit plans, and so forth. They also understand that working together substantially advances the development of intellectual/professional capital (i.e., development of learning programs, standards, and performance measurements). Unless smaller partnerships work together, the burden in human time and talent and in financial terms is too great to keep up with larger organizations. Trying to do everything in a small partnership leads to burnout.

To address these realities, cooperatives often form service organizations, physician groups form management services organizations; schools create educational services organizations; and farmers form agricultural cooperatives. Each of these organizations is created with the express purpose of serving the needs of the entities that created them. Often these service organizations are governed by the entities they serve.

Many small TPPs will want to outsource some administrative and business activities and may find it advantageous to create or partner with a service organization. Charter schools that do not have a TPP may have needs very similar to TPPs, and TPPs may want to form an organization with charter schools. They may also avail themselves of existing education service organizations.

A TPP must purchase many services, depending on the expertise and time commitments of its members. Typically, a service organization will offer a menu of services, some of which all member organizations will use, and some of which only some organizations will choose to use. A service organization should consider offering some or all of the following services:

Administrative Services
- Payroll
- Accounting

- State report preparation
- Purchasing insurance
- Pension plan administration
- Personnel systems
- Purchasing technology and other goods/supplies

Professional Support/Development Services
- Common measurement system
- Learning program development
- Peer review program suggestions
- Quality review suggestions
- Learning organization development
- Professional development
- Charter school legislation, etc.
- Educational programs on the nature and creation of TPPs

Teaching Services
- Back-up staff
- Special education
- World languages

The above list is one example of how the services might be classified or divided. The bottom line is that if a TPP is small, some services must be outsourced.

## PROFESSIONAL STANDARDS OF PRACTICE

To be effective, a TPP must articulate clearly the expectations for the teachers it invites to become members of the partnership. The TPP should develop a membership committee that will take the time and steps necessary to create a set of standards and expectations and thoroughly check the backgrounds of potential members.

Accredited institutions of higher education set the standards for licensure of teachers. Therefore, it may be assumed that the licensed teachers considered for membership have met those standards. Also, all licensed teachers have more than likely had criminal background checks. When considering new teachers as members, checking the credentials of the institution and the standards by which they graduate licensed teachers should be a necessary step.

Most institutions that prepare teachers have similar methods and experiences for novice teachers. Not many new teachers are trained in methods other than the behaviorist information delivery model. Some institutions have created programs for individuals who seek a more experiential education or more constructivist approaches, and some novice teachers may have had a clinical experience in a constructivist school. Therefore, it may be necessary to check out the coursework, the standards upon which the student teaching and other clinical experiences are assessed, and whether the state from which the new teachers were licensed requires a basic skills test.

The next obvious step is to check the references offered by the student teacher's university or college supervisor and the references of the classroom supervisor. It is important to call these references and ask direct and specific questions about relationships, methods of instruction, standards and competencies, leadership qualities, and any other qualities that seem relevant.

When considering experienced teachers for membership, it is useful to ask about the mission and vision of their previous schools to see if there is a match. It is wise to check with references to see what philosophy governs the school processes, what methods of instruction are used, and whether the teacher has had experiences as a leader. It is a good practice to call and talk not only with references but also to ask that a new criminal background check be completed. Even though a check was done prior to licensure, it would not be unfair to ask for a background check on potential new partners and associates.

It is also a good practice to ask references about a potential member's attitude toward vision and mission. And it is essential to inquire about whether a potential member has the personality and attitude to make the transition from being an employee to being an owner. Not all teachers can operate in an ownership model.

## Local Standards

The most critical step is to discover whether a potential member is a good fit for the TPP's learning program. Checking credentials and references may not answer all of the relevant questions on the matter. Of course, it is necessary to determine if the individual has had experiences (in any school) that approximate the kind of experiences he or she will have in this new situation. However, if the TPP is involved with an innovative program, experience in the learning program may be very limited. The leaders of the TPP will want to devise a set of questions to address the type of teacher behaviors expected. If the mission and vision are clear and a learning program has been clearly defined, it should not be difficult to devise a set of relevant questions.

For example, the vision of what would make an excellent member for EdVisions Cooperative sites has already been articulated. Because EdVisions Cooperative sites utilize a student-centered, constructivist approach, and because their teacher advisors conduct themselves as owners rather than employees, teacher advisors are required to have skills and competence that not all teachers may possess.

Teachers in EdVisions Cooperative schools are expected to:

- Give up power over others in order to develop self-disciplined independent learners.
- Be self-efficacious in order to build self-efficacy in others.
- Be creative in developing relationships and learning opportunities; be grounded in authenticity and the real world.
- Expand their cognitive horizons and integrate knowledge from other disciplines.
- Articulate the difference between levels of learning and understand that process is more important than content.
- Be reflective and self-analytical about themselves and their teaching.
- Demonstrate that they are lifelong learners.
- Understand that the relationship between student and teacher is one of mentor to novice rather than one of authority figure to antagonist.
- Work with students to establish orderly processes, routines, and procedures and allow students to take responsibility. (Caine and Caine, 1997)

The expectations cited may serve as a model for other TPPs and may serve as a point of departure in ascertaining potential members' understanding and beliefs.

## Staff Development

Ongoing staff development is a must in any organization. It is recommended that a good staff development plan be devised by the TPP for the purpose of ongoing educator growth. In order to accomplish its mission, each individual in an organization should be asked to complete a professional development plan; accept roles and responsibilities in the school or association; work with others to acquire feedback about quality of work and areas of improvement; and develop a habit of personal study and reflection for self-improvement.

Good professional development focuses on teachers as the central link to student learning. In order for teachers to become better at their profession, there should be a focus on nurturing their intellectual and leadership capacity. There should also be a focus on individual, collegial, and organizational improvement. Reflection on best practices as outlined by the best available research is a must. There should always be a focus on the developing of expertise in the particular teaching methods, strategies, and technologies central to the mission of the organization.

Exemplary professional development plans in teacher professional partnerships must show evidence of improved student learning and increased teacher effectiveness. The organization should devise a process for collecting good data on student achievement and teacher effectiveness and should develop a supportive, nonpunitive method of staff observation and peer coaching. If a good set of competencies has been developed (the same set of competencies used for seeking new partners), a process of observation and feedback can be developed from these so that teachers may become more effective in improving student achievement.

Parent and student surveys on teacher effectiveness may be a good tool, but they should never be used by themselves. Professionals should be judged primarily by other professionals. A professional, growth-oriented teacher will be self-reflective and analytical and willing to learn how to best influence student achievement and make the school program better. Reflection requires that each individual teacher look at ways he or she may affect behavior, first his or her own, and second, the behavior of students.

Good staff development requires that teachers have an individual professional development plan. The plan should include peer involvement, for example, two peers who oversee the plans of another colleague. Each organization should create a personnel team to oversee the creation and completion of an annual professional development plan for each member.

It may be useful to create a checklist for professional development plans. One example is the checklist used by EdVisions Cooperative:

- Choose a professional development team of school site personnel.
- Complete a peer evaluation process utilizing observations, surveys, data collected from assessments, and so forth.
- Write an action plan based upon the above and include items such as the following, if they are appropriate to action plan goals:
  - Attend state or national conferences.
  - Attend university or college classes.
  - Do professional reading and reflections approved by the team.
  - Complete relicensure/certification as required.
  - Arrange a year-end interview with the team.
- Collect student data and conduct appropriate feedback surveys.
- Develop two new student experiences/projects/activities.
- Serve on the school board, in the organizational office, or on the lead committee.
- Complete a personal health and wellness plan. (Thomas, 1996)

Staff development activities should always be focused on creating healthier teacher–student and teacher–teacher relationships. The overall mission of staff development is to develop individual responsibility, accountability, and ownership of the educational enterprise to make the school site stronger and healthier. Strong and healthy organizations will enhance the teacher professional partnership's ability to thrive as a business and successful educational enterprise.

## MEMBERSHIP, COMPENSATION, DISTRIBUTION OF INCOME, BUY-INS, AND BUY-OUTS

### Membership and Ownership

As stated earlier, the first step, prior to inviting individuals to become members of the TPP, is to establish a personnel committee. In some cases, this committee may include all of the partners in the TPP. Building on the business plan, this committee needs to articulate clearly the expectations for membership in the partnership, the specific professional needs of the educational endeavor in which the partnership is engaged, the number of persons required to carry out the responsibilities of the partnership, and the process to be used to grant membership in the organization.

What does "membership" in the partnership mean? While different terms may be used to describe being part of a partnership in medicine, accounting, law, workers cooperatives, and consulting, the underlying manner of organizing these practices or partnerships is similar. Professional partnerships have a group of owners, sometimes called partners, principals, shareholders, or members, and may also have a group of associates who are employees. Associate status may be a temporary status while a new professional is in a one or more year evaluation waiting period, or it may be a permanent status, based on the decisions of the professional partnership. Small professional partnerships often have all professional members as owners.

Ownership brings with it the opportunity to be a part of the governance of the organization, to have a vote in the key decisions of the organization, and to share in the organization's earnings. Beyond these obvious attributes of ownership, there is the more intangible, but no less important, attribute of feeling and acting as an owner rather than an employee. Associate or employee status does not bring the benefits of ownership.

TPP members may include credentialed teachers, other professionals, paraprofessionals, and other staff. Typically, only persons involved in the actual work of the partnership are eligible for membership; so parents and individuals in the larger community would not typically be members. A TPP must decide for itself if every professional member will be offered ownership, or if it will have some partners and some employees.

The very purpose—and the power—of establishing TPPs is to encourage education professionals to become owners. For this reason, we encourage the goal of having every professional member become a partner. This naturally requires very careful selection of the individuals to be offered membership and partnership.

In a start-up organization, the founders typically choose to become a teacher professional partnership based on their previous relationships and knowledge of one another. As stated earlier, the initial business plan must articulate the cultural, educational, and business requirements for membership. These requirements will apply to the founders and to any persons brought into the TPP after it is operational. The founders typically become owners without any waiting period. When new persons are needed in the TPP after it becomes operational, it is important to have a process in place to offer ownership. Many partnerships will have an evaluation waiting period of one, two, or three years for prospective members. The purpose of the evaluation waiting period is to determine if the new person is a good fit, from both the individual and the partnership's perspective. During the evaluation waiting period, this individual is an employee of the partnership.

## Peer Review

We have mentioned peer review many times in this guide. (See chapter 3, section entitled "Culture and Leadership"; and above, in "Professional Standards of Practice.") We have recommended the establishment of a personnel team or committee to champion and oversee professional development in the TPP. We also recommend that each individual have an annual professional development plan, established in conjunction with the committee. The committee, or some members of the committee, performs a periodic peer review with each member of the TPP. It is important that these reviews be conducted in the spirit of continuous improvement and professional development.

Peer review is often one of the most difficult tasks faced by a professional partnership. Since it is difficult, it is often done poorly. Poor peer review may result in lack of accountability, slow professional growth, low morale, and poor organizational performance.

## Compensation

One of the most important opportunities—and burdens—of a TPP is that the partners set compensation. Neither the teachers union nor the school board determines salaries or benefits for a TPP. Partners determine the salary for each person and the amount of compensation to be used for pensions and other benefits. They also pick the health plan and other insurance plans. They determine vacation and sick leave policies. Discussions about compensation have the potential to be difficult and divisive. It is important for the TPP to establish a process that every partner perceives to be fair.

The positive part of this arrangement, however, is that the partners are in control. When the budget is established, the partners determine exactly how much of the budget will be used for instructional compensation, for administrative compensation, and for other purposes. They may use whatever formula(s) they choose to determine individual compensation. The challenge here is that setting compensation is very difficult because it is a matter each member of the organization takes seriously and personally.

It is important to note here, as well, that some members may be asked to take on leadership and/or management/administrative responsibilities. Compensation for these activities will need to be factored into the plan.

## Distribution of Income

At the end of the year, the TPP may have earnings or excess income. Costs may have been lower than expected, or there may have been more students than anticipated. The TPP partners will need to decide what to do with any excess income. The business plan and the annual budget process will alert the TPP to the need to have a contingency fund. Also, as in any business, there is a need to retain some earnings to have funds available for expansion or development of the partnership.

Typically, professional partnerships make a decision before the end of the tax year to pay some of the excess earnings in the form of compensation. This compensation is an operating cost of the TPP and not a year-end profit. To the extent that there is a profit, that is, earnings in excess of all costs, there may be tax consequences to the organization. As outlined in the first section of this chapter on the various options for a TPP's legal structure, one of the most important considerations in choosing a legal structure is the different tax treatments of profits.

## Buy-Ins and Buy-Outs

An owner is, by definition, someone who has an ownership interest in the TPP. There are several ways in which a person may obtain an ownership interest. These include purchasing or being given shares of stock as compensation for services rendered or to be rendered. A purchase may be made over a period of years through payroll deduction.

There are two fundamental reasons for requiring a personal financial investment or an investment of services rendered or to be rendered in order to obtain an ownership interest. The first is to provide working capital for the organization. The partnership's business plan will detail the needs for working capital and the potential sources of funds. A TPP may or may not have the bulk of its working capital needs met without a cash investment by the owners. It is also possible that initial planning will require funds derived from a cash investment made by the owners.

The second reason—and this is fundamental—is that the act of using and risking some of one's own money makes the whole concept of a TPP and ownership more real. The TPP will be taken more seriously if some financial investment is required.

How should a TPP determine the level of the investment, and are there any parameters? The obvious answer is that, as stated above, there must be sufficient capital. The level of investment must be attainable by the initial partners and anyone invited to become a partner in the future. The TPP is free to decide for itself what the level of investment needs to be. The TPP may also decide whether the purchase of an ownership interest can be made over a period of time.

In addition to developing a process for the acquisition of an ownership interest by persons founding or joining the TPP, there must also be a process to deal with persons who cease being partners because they choose to leave or because the TPP asks them to leave. The TPP will need sufficient funds to purchase the investment interest of those who leave the partnership. The TPP will also need to protect itself from a situation in which many partners decide to leave at the same time. Often investment interests are redeemed over a period of time to alleviate a drain on the organization's funds.

TPPs should seek legal and business advice to deal with these issues.

## OPTIONS FOR FRINGE BENEFITS

### State-Sponsored Teacher Retirement Plans

The availability of teacher retirement programs will be a very important issue for teachers considering joining or forming a TPP. One option that may be available to the partnership is participation in a state-
sponsored teacher retirement program. However, significant legal
issues may arise concerning members of a TPP participating in state-
sponsored programs. The eligibility requirements for state-sponsored
programs will vary from state to state. Furthermore, there is a critical
interrelationship between state-sponsored programs and applicable
federal law. Accordingly, the TPP should obtain competent legal advice
concerning participation in a state-sponsored program and the possible
implications of participation for both the members of the TPP and the
retirement program itself.

As an alternative to participating in a state-sponsored program, the
TPP may wish to, or be required to, design its own retirement program.
Such programs are common in other professions and may provide the
partnership with greater flexibility in designing a benefit package to
meet the needs of the TPP and its members. An independent program
such as this will also avoid any serious legal issues associated with participating in a state-sponsored teacher retirement program.

### Private Retirement Plan Options

Members of TPPs have several options for developing retirement
plans. These plans are all qualified retirement plans, that is, plans must
meet standards established in federal law and regulations. Appendix B
contains an overview of six private plans available to organizations such
as TPPs. It is useful to understand each option's advantages and disadvantages. TPP members should seek professional guidance to help
choose the option that meets the objectives of its members.

### Advantages and Disadvantages of Private Retirement Plans

Some teachers find the change from a state-sponsored retirement
plan to a private plan to be the hurdle that keeps them from considering

a TPP. The truth is that private plans have advantages, as well as disadvantages:

Advantages
- TPPs may choose to allow immediate vesting.
- TPPs may contribute a larger amount to members' retirement plans than would be the case under a state sponsored plan.
- In most options members may contribute their own money in addition to TPP contributions, thereby building an even larger fund.
- Typically, individual members can choose how their money is invested from a choice of very conservative fixed income investments to a variety of kinds of equities.
- Private plans are portable. If a member leaves the TPP, he or she can roll over 100 percent of the vested money into a new retirement account controlled by the member.
- Private plans are quite flexible.
- Properly designed, a private plan does not create "golden handcuffs," as some public retirement plans do. The member is not tied to the organization only because too much would be forfeited on leaving.

Disadvantages
- Private plans are defined contribution plans. That is, the retirement benefit is a product of the amount of money contributed by the TPP and the member, plus the growth in the funds through the market performance of the investment options chosen. There is more risk in a private plan, but there is also the potential for more reward, especially over the long run. Currently, state-sponsored plans are likely to be defined benefit plans. That is, they are designed to provide retirees a specified portion of their salary as a retirement benefit. The benefit is usually tied to longevity. Often public bodies will periodically adjust the retirement payments for inflation once a recipient begins to receive benefits.
- Teachers with a great deal of seniority may hesitate to leave a state-sponsored plan. State-sponsored retirement plan benefits are frequently designed to be much more generous to persons who stay for their entire or a great portion of their career (i.e., a set of "golden handcuffs").

## Purchasing Insurance Coverage

TPPs need to provide coverage for health, dental, disability, and liability insurance based on the members' preferences and choices. Small businesses such as TPPs may purchase small group insurance. However, they will often find it advantageous to be part of a larger network or service organization that can purchase insurance for a large group.

We recommend above that several TPPs combine to form a purchasing organization, which will enable them to achieve the economies of scale and purchasing power of a larger organization (see above, "Partnership Size and Service Organizations"). Creating such an organization is an excellent way to approach insurance coverage.

# WHAT ARE THE IMPLICATIONS?

As we explained in the opening pages of this guide, teacher ownership is not *the* answer, but *one* answer to the problems confronting education. However, teacher ownership has enormous implications for the national conversation about public education. In this chapter we address some of the implications for teachers, students, parents, and the broader community; buyers of TPP services (clients); teachers unions; teacher education; education policy; and policymakers. We offer these ideas with the understanding that others will have valuable insights to add to the discussion.

## IMPLICATIONS FOR TEACHERS, STUDENTS, PARENTS, AND THE COMMUNITY

Teacher professional partnerships create major changes in the basic arrangement of authority and responsibility in the schools, and these changes, in turn, create major implications for the key stakeholders of the schools. The lessons learned from existing TPPs, as well as from the partnerships of professionals in other fields, shed light on the implications of this model for teachers, students, parents, and the broader community. The implications cited here are not exhaustive, but they are indicative of the scope and range of the possibilities a TPP approach can bring to school governance.

## Potential Changes for Teachers

Participating in the ownership and operation of a TPP has a profound impact on the professional lives of the teacher owners. Teachers in these partnerships move from focusing mainly on their particular classes and students to the broader view that comes from being in control of all aspects of the school or program. Teachers need to move from thinking mainly about curriculum and instruction to being involved with and responsible for the overall school climate, the budget, personnel, and all other aspects of the operation.

Some of the changes that teachers may experience include:

- Freedom to design or choose a learning program.
- Ability to choose colleagues (co-owners) as well as leaders (both whom and how many).
- Decreased turnover.
- A greater opportunity to shape and implement a shared culture (vision, mission, and values).
- Greater personal control over and responsibility for day-to-day operations that affect their professional lives.
- An expanded sense of challenge, creativity, and accomplishment.
- Direct responsibility for participating in budget decisions that trade-off compensation, benefits, program enhancements, technology, program administration, and other trade-offs.
- An opportunity to create processes that are less confrontational and more efficient.
- Greater stability in the professional environment.
- Greater accountability, shared liability, and a requirement to continuously achieve high levels of professional development.
- No tenure, no guarantees, a greater reliance on demonstrated competence for security.
- More interdependence with other professionals, parents, community, and students.

- A requirement to take more personal responsibility for high levels of student performance and service to students and parents.
- A need to assume the responsibility for the successful operation of the business, the overall school or program, as well as individual student learning.

## Potential Changes for Students

Students who participate in a program or school operated by a TPP will also find differences in their experience. These differences will be the result of changes in the behavior of the adults (mainly the teachers).

Some of the changes that students may experience include:

- A more cohesive and integrated sense of purpose, goals, and measurements of success.
- A greater sense of involvement in and responsibility for the school or program.
- More immediate feedback and problem resolution.
- A greater sense of partnership with the teachers in the learning activities.
- More innovative and varied learning opportunities.
- Increased opportunity to use new information technology.
- More individual attention.
- A requirement for greater parental involvement.
- Higher expectations for students and a requirement that students accept greater responsibility for their learning.

## Potential Changes for Parents

Teachers who own the business clearly understand that they are accountable for student performance, and realize that the future of their business is tied to student success. They will look to every possible resource to assist in the effort to improve student learning. They are more likely than teachers who are employees of a district (with a governing board, a superintendent, and building principals) to actively involve parents and the broader community.

Some of the changes that parents and the broader community may experience include:

- Expectations for active involvement in student learning and school or program activities.
- A greater sense of involvement in and belonging to the school or program.
- Improved student performance.
- More immediate feedback and problem resolution.
- An ability to attract and keep good teachers.
- Higher expectations for the use of new information technology.
- An expectation that students will accept greater responsibility for their learning.
- A more cohesive and integrated sense of purpose, goals, and measurement of success.
- More frequently articulated purpose, goals, and measurement of success.
- Use of innovative learning programs to serve individual student needs and aptitudes.
- An understanding that there is no long-term guarantee that the school or program will continue to operate.
- Acceptance (by parents, students, and communities) that occasionally a TPP will fail and will cease to exist.

These changes may seem profound, and these implications may appear formidable to significant portions of each of these stakeholder groups. However, even limited experience with this new set of arrangements suggests that there is strong interest on the part of a substantial numbers of teachers, parents, and students in experiencing the kind of schools and programs that result from the teacher ownership model. Expanding examples and variations of this model will create an opportunity to determine whether the TPP approach can improve student learning, something that has eluded public education in this country for the past quarter century.

## IMPLICATIONS FOR CHARTER SCHOOL AND DISTRICT SCHOOL BOARDS CONTRACTING WITH TPPs

For charter or district school boards, contracting with a TPP promises to clarify the often murky distinctions between school governance and management, between "steering" and "rowing." A charter school board or school district board that contracts with a TPP is no longer the employer of everyone in the school or department, with all of the attendant legal and financial challenges and responsibilities. Nor is the board dependent on one administrator whose personal strengths and limitations will determine the performance and direction of the organization in ways that a board may find difficult to influence. The unwise temptation of the board to micromanage should be lessened as roles become clearer. Perhaps most importantly, contracting with a strong TPP should help free a school board to focus exclusively on the core governance function of ensuring school performance, accountability, and fidelity to its mission. The discussion that follows begins with a review of the implications for charter school boards and ends with a review of implications for school districts and their boards.

### Understanding Roles and Responsibilities

A charter school board should have a clear understanding of its own roles and responsibilities before contracting with a TPP—or operating a school in any form. As adapted from the list of core responsibilities outlined by the National Center for Nonprofit Boards, charter school boards must:

- Determine and ensure adherence to the school's mission and purpose.
- Select, support, evaluate, and, if necessary, replace the school's administrator.
- Ensure effective organizational planning.
- Ensure adequate resources and manage resources effectively.
- Determine and monitor the performance of the school's programs and services.

- Enhance the school's public image.
- Ensure compliance with applicable local, state, and federal laws and regulations.
- Ensure effective communications and strong relationships among all stakeholders.
- Ensure responsiveness to the school's customers, consistent with its mission.
- Assess and improve the board's own performance. (*Creating an Effective Charter School Governing Board,* 2000)

If, instead of hiring an administrator who in turn hires teacher employees, the charter school board decides to contract with a TPP to manage and implement the learning program, only the wording of the second item on the list above would change: "Select, support, evaluate, and, if necessary, replace the school's TPP." For charter schools, the leading resource on the roles and responsibilities of boards is the Charter Friends National Network's *Creating An Effective Charter School Governing Board* (2000), a comprehensive 350-page manual.

The TPP becomes the agent of the charter school board in carrying out the learning program and other services, as specified in the contract. In effect, the board's main role becomes the procurer and monitor of contracts with external service providers.

At Avalon School, a St. Paul, Minnesota, charter high school that opened in the fall of 2001, the charter school board oversaw at least five separate contracts by the end of its first operating year (Bacal, 2001). These contracts were made with a:

- Teachers cooperative (or TPP) to run the learning program of the school.
- Charter start-up consulting firm to provide planning, governmental, facilities, fundraising, and other start-up support during the pre-opening phase.
- Separate entity that is the school's landlord.
- Local YMCA to provide recreational services.
- Staff development and school evaluation consultant—functions of both TPP and board.

## Key Questions for the Charter School Board

Before contracting with a TPP or any other entity, the charter school board should consult the Charter Friends National Network guide *Charting a Clear Course: A Resource Guide for Charter Schools Contracting with School Management Organizations* (2001). Minnesota School Board Association's *Fundamentals of School Board Membership: A Guide for Newly-Elected Charter School Board Members* (1998) is also a useful reference. Assuming the charter school board is aware of its own governance roles and responsibilities, it should ask and answer the following questions before contracting with a TPP:

- What is the market of service providers? Among an increasingly diverse marketplace of various potential TPPs, education management organizations and traditional principals, which will be a good philosophical and practical fit our mission and the needs of customers/ families/students? What are the financial implications of different choices? The board must be a smart shopper.
- What are the specific roles and responsibilities of the TPP versus the board's own desired role in budgeting, compliance, student recruitment, and fundraising.
- How long will the contract last and under what conditions may the parties terminate or renew the relationship?
- How will the performance of the TPP be evaluated? *Charting a Clear Course* suggests that an agreed upon evaluation plan include:
  - Clear, specific, measurable annual goals for student learning at all grade levels.
  - The instruments and measures that will be used to assess student learning.
  - Methods and timelines for oversight, evaluation, and intervention.
- Precisely how will the financial affairs be managed? How are surpluses, deficits, lines of credit, and debts handled?
- In the event of contract termination, how will an orderly transition be managed, and how will physical and intellectual property be divided?

## Two Charter School Board Approaches to TPP Contracting

Under the most direct approach, a charter school board establishes a contract with a TPP, which is given control of a significant portion of the whole budget or the whole learning program budget. The TPP is responsible for selection, determining the compensation of, and managing its own partners—the teachers of the school. The charter school board's role is limited to monitoring the performance of the school and the TPP and deciding whether and under what terms to renew the TPP at the end of the year.

A second approach is more incremental. Strongly committed to the TPP model, the board of the new Avalon School in St. Paul, Minnesota, currently considers the set of teachers they have just hired to be "employees" of the board. However, all of Avalon's teachers are committed to forming a TPP or to becoming members of a multischool teachers' cooperative early in the school's first year (2001–2002). In the meantime, they are working closely with the charter school board on budgeting and other key matters. Well before the end of the year, Avalon's teachers will collectively contract with Avalon's school board as a single TPP rather than as individual employees. Until then, however, the charter school board will retain formal control over monthly budgeting, personnel, and other decisions.

Avalon School adopted this approach in order to give its teachers—none of whom has TPP experience—time to learn and organize themselves in a first-year school, while giving its board a greater degree of control during its critical first year. As a new member of the Gates EdVisions project, Avalon and its teachers are receiving training and support from the team behind Minnesota New Country School and other EdVisions Cooperative members in order to replicate the Edvisions Cooperative approach.

## Establishing an Arm's-Length Relationship Between TPPs and Charter School Boards

The ultimate presumed and required precondition to contracting with a TPP, to paraphrase *Charting a Clear Course* (2001), is the establishment of an arm's-length, performance-based relationship between the board and the TPP. Establishing an arm's-length relationship can be particularly challenging and complex in the event that the board members of a school include (or are mainly composed of) members of the TPP. The charter law of Minnesota, the birthplace of charter schools, mandates that a majority of the membership of charter school boards be composed of teachers who work at the school (there is now a provision for a waiver from that provision).

A charter school board must have clear policies, procedures, and structures in place to ensure arm's-length relationships and avoid possible conflicts of interest. These policies might include:

- Creating subcommittees of noninterested members to handle decisions where some board members have a conflict.
- Requiring interested board members to remove themselves from certain decisions.
- Prohibiting TPP members on the charter school board from a role in selecting any board members or from a role in selecting non–TPP board members.
- Fully disclosing potential conflicts in board discussions, minutes, and annual reports.
- Requiring the approval of the charter school's authorizer or other objective, neutral authority before contracting or renewing a contract with a TPP whose membership overlaps with the charter school board.
- Intentionally limiting board discretion by establishing clear, measurable, and mutually agreed upon performance benchmarks for the TPP and preventing the renewal of the TPP contract if these benchmarks have not been met. To a considerable extent, the board's relationship to the TPP should parallel the charter authorizer's ideal relationship to a charter school: freedom for the TPP regarding means in exchange for real accountability for results.

In any event, if the charter school board and TPP membership overlaps, the TPP members who serve on the board should be especially conscious of the governance role they must play in board meetings.

## Implications for School District Boards

While contracting for instruction by school district boards of education has been rare, there are indications that superintendents and boards are increasingly attracted to contracting as a method of encouraging a focus on results rather than inputs and as a method of attracting and retaining entrepreneurial educators. Districts could contract with a group of teachers organized as a TPP to run a new or existing school, a department of a school, or a districtwide program (e.g., the secondary math or alternative program) across multiple sites. Teachers might themselves propose a new school to the board for charter or contract status or to propose converting an existing school. The board might take the initiative to form a school and ask teachers to run the school as a TPP.

Like the charter TPP arrangements outlined earlier, for working with TPPs district boards of education should focus on their core governance responsibilities. These include:

- Approving a proposal from the TPP that outlines how the TPP will run the school or program, including how the financial affairs will be managed.
- Measuring the results of the program annually, based on a set of objectives, reasonable benchmarks and indicators that have been mutually agreed upon by the TPP and the board at the beginning, and linking renewal of the arrangement to the TPP's progress in reaching these benchmarks.
- Avoiding the natural temptation of boards to micromanage the operations of the school or program; avoiding the temptation to allow political considerations to interfere with the evaluation of the arrangement.

(For additional guidelines in this area, see the Education Commission of the States' report *National Commission on Governing America's Schools*, 1999; Paul T. Hill's article "Charter School Districts," published in 2001 by the Progressive Policy Institute; *Reinventing Public Education: How Contracting Can Transform America's Schools* (1997), a book by Paul T. Hill, Lawrence C. Pierce, and James W. Guthrie.) Like the decision to hire an individual for the position of school principal, the decision to contract with a TPP must be made after a careful screening and selection process, a consideration of key questions, and a candid, in-depth exploration by both parties of the terms, philosophies, potential conflicts, contingencies, and challenges.

## IMPLICATIONS FOR TEACHERS UNIONS

As we consider the implications of TPPs for teachers unions, it seems useful to briefly review the conditions surrounding teachers and teaching during the twentieth century. In the early years of the twentieth century most teachers were young women, many of them starting their teaching careers while they were still teenagers. The professional training for these young women was quite minimal, usually not more than two years of post high school learning.

All through the twentieth century the professional training expected for a career in teaching has escalated. But until the 1960s, the vast majority of teachers still had no control over, or even meaningful input into, the decisions about the practice of their profession. The decisions about compensation and other conditions of employment, as well as all decisions about personnel selection and evaluation, organization of the school, and selection of learning programs, were made unilaterally by governing boards or administrators hired by the governing boards. For a variety of reasons this approach to decision making began to gradually change during the 1960s. The increase in professional training, the influx of ex-GI's trained under the GI Bill, and the increase of young teachers hired to teach the children of the baby boom all contributed to the growing pressure for more teacher involvement in decision making in the schools.

During this period, a large percentage of teachers joined one of the two national teachers organizations and became increasingly assertive in the political arena. Later, during the 1960s and 1970s, most states enacted legislation making collective bargaining for teachers legal. While these legal changes were considered major achievements, many of these laws made compensation and conditions of employment legitimate items for the bargaining process but left as "management rights" such issues as the selection and evaluation of personnel, the organization of schools, and the selection and implementation of learning programs. These legal changes provided for significant involvement by teachers in the decisions regarding compensation and other conditions of employment and have led to substantial improvement in these areas for teachers over the past forty or so years. The other half of the professional equation, the right to meaningful involvement in the decisions about issues, now considered "management rights," continues to elude teachers and to be the exclusive authority of the governing boards and their administrators.

The opportunity for teachers to create, join, and operate professional partnerships provides an opportunity for teachers to experience the full range of decision-making authority that has always existed for members of the legal and medical professions. The decisions about school calendars, learning programs, allocation of budgets, compensation, and the hiring and evaluation of personnel are decisions that teachers have sought for years. Consequently, the opportunity to participate in TPPs will fulfill a long-sought goal for teachers. On the other hand, if teachers form and join TPPs, they will usually become owners of the business. It is legitimate, then, to ask why such teachers would need a union to represent their interests with the employer when *they* are the employer.

While the development of TPPs presents teachers and their unions with the opportunity to realize some of their long-sought goals, this development will require some fundamental changes in the way teachers unions operate. Some teachers union leaders are aware of the importance of their leadership in changing the education landscape. The Teachers Union Reform Network (TURN), an organization of some of the most progressive teachers union leaders in the country, was formed on the premise that unions have to be involved in leading the transformation of education in America.

There are at least two approaches that unions should consider if the development of TPPs spreads. One approach would have the union decide to provide an array of professional and other services to TPP members that does not include bargaining for their compensation and conditions of employment. Albert Shanker stated in a private conversation in 1988 that bargaining is not an essential feature of unions (Kolderie, 1988). Members of TPPs will have need for a strong advocate for the teaching profession, as well as the usual strong advocacy for adequate funding for public education. It seems reasonable to assume that if an existing organization does not come forward to provide this advocacy for TPPs and their members, a new organization will need to be created in order to carry out these functions.

Members of TPPs will also need a variety of services that could easily be provided by unions or a new variation of unions. Retirement programs, other fringe benefits, and professional development services are some examples. A very high percentage of attorneys and doctors belong to organizations in their professions (comparable to teachers unions) for the purpose of advancement of the profession and for receiving services other than collective bargaining. It is useful to remember that a similarly high percentage of teachers belonged to one of the major teacher organizations before these organizations received the right to collectively bargain for their members. In undertaking this approach, it would probably be desirable for union leaders not to attempt to change the existing organization but to establish a new subsidiary organization to provide these services to teachers in TPPs.

It may also be possible to create arrangements that allow teachers to participate in TPPs and continue to be members of a local teachers union. The United Teachers of Dade (Florida) is in the process of starting several charter schools. Its plan is to contract with the Dade Board of Education for the teachers who will teach in these charter schools. The teachers will be employees of the board of education and covered by the collective bargaining agreement between the United Teachers of Dade and the Dade Board of Education while they are teaching in the charter school. This model does not, at this time, involve the creation of a TPP, but it does provide a model for how partners might retain their union membership.

In Milwaukee, Wisconsin, I.D.E.A.L. Charter School was established under the "Instrumentality Charter School" arrangement (See appendix D "Emerging Model"). This arrangement allows the teachers to remain as employees of the district and, therefore, to be subject to the provisions of the bargaining agreement. A separate legal entity, I.D.E.A.L. Charter School Cooperative was created by the teachers, which they own and control. Through this entity the teachers will exercise control of all professional aspects of the school. The entity will manage the school, including the learning program and other aspects. There is a memorandum of understanding between the charter school and the union regarding flexibility on some of the issues in the master contract. In this instance, the teachers will have their compensation established by the collective bargaining agreement and will still be employees of the district, but they will be owners of the entity, and through this entity will exercise control over the other aspects of their practice. One of the major distinctions between the Dade initiative and the Milwaukee effort is that, in Dade, it is the union that is creating the charters, while in Milwaukee, the initiative is coming from a group of union members working with the union and the board of education. These types of arrangements will test whether the cultures of teacher ownership and union involvement are compatible in the same organization.

As we enter the early years of a new century, the landscape in which public education operates is undergoing substantial change. The growing importance of knowledge in our society, the escalating expectations on our schools by business leaders, political leaders, and the general public all contribute to a sense of urgency in the efforts to attain significant improvement in student achievement in our public schools. TPPs represent an innovation that provides the opportunity for teachers to finally achieve the professional control of their work that they have sought throughout the twentieth century and into the twenty-first.

## IMPLICATIONS FOR TEACHER EDUCATION

The development of opportunities for teachers to create and participate in TPPs will present some significant challenges in the area of teacher education, both at the preservice level and in continuing education. A substantial amount of existing teacher education will continue to be important to teachers regardless of the nature of the governance structure of the schools in which they practice. For example, the growing body of knowledge about developmental psychology, experimental pedagogy, and best practices will continue to be important to all teachers (Cohen, 1999). The teachers practicing as partners in a TPP will, of course, require additional skills in order to be successful contributors to their partnerships. Since the bulk of new teachers will continue to start their careers in the traditional system, it seems likely that for the near future the additional knowledge and skills needed by members of a TPP will have to be provided as continuing education. Eventually the number of TPPs may grow to the point that it becomes feasible to substantially alter preservice programs.

As this transition takes place, providing these teacher education services to the profession will be difficult for teacher education programs. Most schools of education have a strong culture that has developed around the assumption that teachers will be employees. Constructing the learning experiences needed to provide the new skills and knowledge for teacher owners will require some creativity and a willingness to break with past practices. Very few, if any, of the faculty in our schools of education have had any experience as teacher owners, and almost none will have had any formal education in the skills and knowledge needed by teacher owners. Consequently, if schools of education are going to position themselves to provide this new type of professional development, they will need to find faculty who are willing to develop this knowledge. Alternatively, they may choose to go to outside sources, perhaps to teachers who are operating TPPs or to other schools within academia, for the faculty expertise needed by teachers who will work in this type of partnership. State teacher licensing authorities will also experience pressure for change, since they will need to decide whether this new knowledge should be a part of preservice or continuing education.

This transition in the practice of teaching, assuming there are a substantial number of teachers creating and practicing in TPPs, will present serious financial issues for the schools of education, as well. It is likely that there will need to be a dual track for teacher development for the foreseeable future, and this will affect the relative efficiencies of the current system. More significant, however, is the likely impact of teacher ownership on the compensation system that is common today. TPPs in which the teachers have control of their own compensation will likely migrate to some sort of compensation system that differs from the traditional "step and lane" system.

The current prevailing step and lane compensation system creates a strong incentive for teachers to go back to graduate school for further education. If compensation systems emerge that significantly alter these traditional incentives, schools of education that provide graduate-level teacher education will certainly be affected. While this type of learning remains necessary, many teachers might find it more desirable to develop new skills and knowledge by going to other types of providers.

In attempting to deal with these kinds of change, it may be necessary for schools of education to create special units to meet the new and emerging needs of teachers who are practicing in the new type of school governance structure. Recent research in the field of organizational change suggests that it will be very difficult to successfully meet the needs of this new market by using the same processes and culture that exists in most of our schools of education today (Chistensen, 2000; Foster and Kaplan, 2001). Meeting the needs of this emerging market will probably require a new organizational space that allows for the major changes in teacher preparation discussed below. If the use of TPPs expands substantially, there will be major benefits to the teacher preparation units that are able to effectively and efficiently meet these new needs.

The additional learning required for members of TPPs falls under the general areas of community, leadership, and management. It seems clear that in actual practice there will be some differentiation of work in the TPPs, but all of the teachers should have the necessary knowledge and skills in these areas. The environment, the place where teachers work with learners must be a learning community. The development of collaborative, competent, self-reliant citizens requires learning communities that are intentionally constructed and sustained. As teachers move into the role of making all decisions about the operation of their school, the importance of creating an effective community will be intensified. Developing and maintaining such communities requires teachers who understand organizational development and the attitudes and skills needed by all stakeholders (parents, teachers, students) for learning and working collaboratively and productively. Community is understood to include all aspects of the school and the larger community in which the school exists.

Teacher ownership means that every individual who works in the school must possess some leadership capability, since all decisions are in the hands of the partners. Moving from the employee model to assuming the responsibilities for creating, leading, and operating a school will require that teachers possess significant additional skills and knowledge. At least some of the teachers will need to possess the ability to think creatively and futuristically about the type of school they will create and operate. Providing effective leadership in a setting of shared ownership will, of course, require strong commitment to shared leadership. Effective leadership requires the assumption of operating ethically and responsibly and skills in group decision making and conflict resolution. Effective leadership requires a long-term commitment to self-renewal through professional growth, both personally and as a community.

The creation of and participation in TPPs will also require that teachers possess substantial knowledge and skills in the area of school management. Facilities acquisition and management, budgeting and finance, accounting and reporting, personnel management and school law are just some of the areas in which teachers will need to possess knowledge and skills that are not included in the usual teacher education programs. Existing teacher education really does not contemplate the teacher as either a leader or as a manager, except as a classroom manager. These areas of expertise and responsibility are assumed to be the province of either the principal or superintendent, and this type of training is therefore provided only in the training for these administrative positions.

Developing and providing the educational experiences necessary for prospective teachers to acquire the knowledge and skills needed in the areas of community, leadership, and management will be a serious challenge. Of course, one of the desired outcomes of moving to TPPs is that they will result in the development and implementation of new, creative, and diversified learning programs—learning programs that fundamentally alter the roles of teachers, students, and parents. If this goal is realized, then the whole of preservice and continuing education for teachers will have to undergo substantial revision beyond the changes discussed above. With this type of future, it is possible to envision teacher preparation with specializations in various types of learning programs, rather than, or perhaps in addition to, the subject area specializations that we now have.

It is also worth considering some of the likely effects of TPPs on teacher expectations for providers of teacher education. Teachers who are members of a TPP are likely to insist on a more active role in the design, evaluation, and operation of both preservice and continuing teacher education programs. This new partnership approach will create teachers who are confident leaders, professionals who have undertaken the creation of purposeful communities that lead to the cocreation of meaning and knowledge. They are likely to expect the same type of experience and preparation for the teachers who will join their partnership. The same sort of characteristics required by business for twenty-first century workers—perpetual learners, team players, individuals who are respectful of diversity and who are open to change—will increasingly be consonant with the expectation for and of educators.

The implications for teacher education become immense when we consider these changes along with the changes needed for effective participation in TPPs. It is clear that the expansion of TPPs will eventually have a profound impact on teacher education programs in the United States.

## IMPLICATIONS FOR EDUCATION
## POLICY AND POLICYMAKERS

The idea of teacher ownership will be a new idea to most of the people engaged in the education policy discussion, and new ideas are often perceived to be problematic. New thinking may not fit easily into existing frameworks and becomes accepted only as people develop new frameworks of thinking. New ideas grow in acceptance, too, as people come to understand how they will make a difference by solving problems that cannot be solved within existing frameworks. As a new idea, teacher ownership faces these hurdles.

The framework for thinking about the issues in public education today is the district framework: a public utility, organized as a bureau, with the teachers as its employees. This notion prevails both outside and inside the institution. The people who work in public education have little experience with other institutions. Many have worked in this institution throughout their entire careers: lateral recruitment is not common. As a result, there is a fairly narrow framework for the policy discussion, a tendency to reject ideas not presently known within the institution, and a tendency to think that ideas outside the experience of K–12 education are somehow odd, however common in other areas of society.

People are unlikely to move out of this old framework unless there are clear and compelling reasons to do so; in this case, unless they can see the difference that teacher ownership would make and see that this difference is important. Teacher ownership does, in fact, have large implications. To appreciate these implications we need to understand them in relationship to the problems of public education today and to the inability of the institution to solve its present problems.

In what follows we identify five important problem areas and then consider how these might change if the idea of ownership were substituted for employment.

## Problem Areas

### *"Getting to Scale" with the Improvement of Learning*

Public education needs to do better—and not just in a few districts, a few schools, and a few classrooms, however exemplary. These efforts appear and last for a while but ultimately fade away as leadership changes or as the grant support runs out.

Improvement needs to last, and improvement needs to spread. For those thinking and worrying seriously about the future of public education, the goal is not simply to make some improvements, good models replicated here and there, little points of light appearing then disappearing. The goal is to develop a continuing *process* of improvement, to make K–12 education self-improving. This is the problem known as "getting to scale."

The leadership in public education affirms the need to do better. The question, the issue—as always—is method. How does the system change? And what should the state do?

The common experience has been that efforts to change do not last and do not spread, especially efforts to change the core of teaching and learning. Larry Cuban at Stanford University, Richard Elmore of the Harvard Graduate School of Education, and others have long described change in education as waves sweeping across the surface of the institution, affecting almost everything but the practices deep inside (Elmore, 1996; Cuban, 1984, 1990). These practices involve, most importantly, teachers' tendency, as Elmore writes, "to think of knowledge as discrete bits of information; of learning as students acquiring these bits of knowledge through a process of repetition, memorization and testing of recall; and of the teacher's role as the center of attention in the classroom, initiating most of the discussion and orchestrating most of the interaction, around brief factual questions, if indeed there is any discussion at all" (1996). These old practices are ineffective with much of today's student population. If learning is to improve these practices at the core, schooling must be changed.

There is a strong desire now to hold students to a higher standard of performance. Increasingly, they are being tested and told they cannot receive a diploma if they have not mastered the academic work. The assumption is that this will cause them to work harder and to learn more. In fact, however, many students, and especially those whose performance we most want to improve, simply quit. In big cities it is common for half or more of the freshmen not to graduate within four years. And this is to be expected. Even if students understand the importance of graduating, the low-grade work they are given to do does not motivate them to make the effort required.

A successful effort to improve student learning will be about improving student motivation. If students want to learn, they will. If they do not want to learn, schools probably cannot make them learn. Motivation is an individual matter because abilities and interests differ. So motivation will require schools to adapt teaching to these differences among students. Teachers cannot do this under present arrangements: curriculum materials are standardized; teachers work mostly with students in groups; teachers are not encouraged—or permitted—to modify the order in which things are taught; and students are not free to pursue topics that interests them. Some teachers do these things behind the classroom door, but outside the rules and with no rewards to offset the risks they run. Many adults in positions of authority believe it is wrong to begin with what interests students.

Within the traditional arrangements it has been virtually impossible to change teacher practices. No experience has successfully demonstrated how to change them, and no theory exists that would make it possible to change them. Elmore ventures a few ideas, but without much conviction. He concludes that, "getting to scale with successful educational practice requires nothing less than deliberately creating and reproducing alternatives to the existing flawed institutional arrangements and incentive structures" (1996). But the policy experts inside the institution, blocked by traditional conceptions, do not have a sense of what these alternatives might be. "There is so little structural variation in American public education . . . that we have little conception what kinds of structures would change the core of teaching" (Elmore, 1996).

## Broadening the Notion of Leadership to Include Teachers

The traditional notion that if one wants to be a teacher one has to be an employee makes it difficult to think of teachers as leaders. Almost by definition, it makes the administrators—the superintendents and principals for whom the teachers work—the leaders. But the days of the "teaching superintendent" are long gone. At the school level the principal (no longer even called "principal teacher") is expected in this single-leader model to be both the manager of the school and the instructional leader.

The effort to develop managers as leaders—on the assumption this would in some way improve student learning—is complicated by the serious and growing problem the institution has in attracting and developing superintendents and principals. Practically no one these days accepts a big-city superintendency twice, and both associations of principals (elementary and secondary) are seriously concerned about the unattractiveness of that job. There are now, as a result, multimillion-dollar efforts by foundations to enlarge the pool of candidates and to develop the skills of leaders. But, again, even though the stated purpose is to improve learning, these efforts have difficulty with the idea of the teacher as a leader, given the assumption of teacher employment (Evans, 2001).

Many thoughtful principals and superintendents see their job as "helping the teachers do their job well." And there is some effort to encourage teachers to "feel ownership" in their job, even though, technically, they are employees, as in the way that in some elite private schools the trustees traditionally let the faculty run the learning side of the school. But the teachers' status as employees constrains such efforts. "Very frankly," the late Arley Gunderman used to say in private discussions, out of his long experience as an elementary school principal and as president of the National Association of Elementary School Principals, "my job is to motivate as much as I can, for as long as I can, people who are in essentially dead-end jobs" (as cited in Kolderie, 1984). There are some principals and superintendents who see teachers as employees who should do what they are told, an impulse currently reinforced by the pressure on superintendents and principals to improve test scores at all costs.

For years, teachers unions have fought to get their members professional status—the right to control "professional issues" within the framework of employment. But to win a kind of shared governance they have had to move through bargaining. Boards have resisted, and at the end of negotiations, money has often been a higher priority for the teachers than professional issues. In some states the unions have tried to persuade the legislature to mandate boards to bargain professional issues, but, not surprisingly, this, too, has been resisted. Boards and their superintendents are not eager to share with employees what they see as their last remaining management rights.

As teachers are blocked from real leadership and decision-making roles about teaching and learning, the problems discussed above are, of course, reinforced.

### Speeding the Take-Up of Technology

There has been growing discussion about the use of new information technologies and new commercial learning programs in the classroom. Progress has been slow, however. Most of the new technologies require changing what teachers do. Especially where these technologies permit the student to work directly on subject matter, they conflict with traditional teaching. It has been hard for administrators to get new, computer-based learning technologies into classrooms where, for a century or more, the dominant technology has been the teacher talking: the two technologies are incompatible. Even where there is a will to change, the problems of teacher training are formidable, as are the problems of keeping up the investment as technologies improve over time.

Even more basic, perhaps, the transition offers little in the way of reward to teachers as employees in return for the effort required. It is not surprising, therefore, that the teachers may choose to ignore or refuse to use new technologies. Teachers are in also in a position to press salary demands that leave little in the budget for the purchase of technology. If money remains, it is sometimes possible to acquire new technology, and administrators do sometimes make the decision to buy. But having the technology does not mean it will be used or used well. More than one district with new technology in the classroom or in the lab has ended up with teachers continuing with what they know and feel comfortable. It would help if there were an incentive for teachers to reach out for and to implement these new technologies themselves. But, so far, that has not happened in K–12 education.

### Increasing the Supply and Quality of Teachers

There is real concern about the supply of teachers, as well as, of course, concern about the quality of that supply. Teaching is a very difficult job, especially as conventionally practiced, with the teacher standing in front of the class talking and struggling, usually, to manage the classroom as a whole. The younger teachers are paid less and are typically assigned to tougher schools, so turnover is relatively high. Districts often find that, at about the five-year point, many teachers drop out. This redirects time and energy toward recruiting.

With the competition for high quality professionals strong from other—and in many cases more attractive—occupations, and with K–12 locked into the assumption of employment in which there is essentially no concept of a teacher getting promoted apart from moving into administration, the institution has a serious problem both attracting and retaining teachers. At the moment, there is also a particular difficulty in paying differentially to attract people to teach in specialty areas where teachers are in short supply. English and/or social studies teachers may be plentiful, while teachers of mathematics and science are hard to find. The single salary scale requires districts to raise the salaries of all teachers in order to be able to attract those in mathematics and science. When raising salaries proves impossible, the positions in mathematics and science cannot be filled with the kind of experienced personnel that districts want and students deserve.

### Financing K–12 Education

The employment arrangement makes it extremely difficult to change the practice and the technology of teaching, but it also has a serious impact on the costs of public education. Unable to "do differently," the institution is blocked from improvements in productivity. Costs continue rise, sometimes at the expense of program. Districts routinely seek grants to pay for improvement and innovation. The increases sought—and often needed—in teacher compensation have a prior claim and come only by voting for tax increases.

This requirement to secure financing politically constrains revenue growth in the system. The essence of public education, some say, is the willingness of people to pay for the education of other people's children. Salaries are bargained; teachers sometimes strike. The public is not always receptive to the images on television of teachers with placards on picket lines. Toward the end of his term as president of the National Education Association, Keith Geiger asked friends, "Do you think we have a problem with bargaining?" To those who said "yes," Geiger is reported to have said that he thought so, too (Kolderie, conversation with Newman). The willingness to bear rising costs is eroded, too, if public education is perceived as an unsuccessful system, if the public begins to resist the assumption implicit in the traditional question: "Would you pay higher taxes to improve the schools?"

Over the years, boards of education have learned that it is better to settle than to take a strike. Under pressure from parents not to cut programs or to raise class size, boards often transfer the cost pressure to the state, joining the teachers in a plea for an increase in aid. But—as public education certainly learned in California—at the state level the appropriations for K–12 will be traded off against the needs of other functions for which the state is responsible, as governors and legislators weigh their appeal against the knowledge that even small percentage increases on what is by far the largest item of state expenditure have huge consequences for the budget and therefore the state's tax requirements.

In the end, both the public's desire for higher quality and the teachers' desire for higher compensation are blocked by the inability to generate improvements in productivity in the system. Yet, under the present arrangements, it is understandable why teachers oppose the actions that might lead to such improvements, since, as employees, they are bound to be skeptical that its benefits would flow substantially to them.

## Addressing Problem Areas through Teacher Ownership

Within the existing framework of K–12 public education there are no satisfactory answers, no satisfactory solutions for these problems—not from experience and not from theory. The traditional givens, most importantly, the commitment to the district idea and to the assumption that teachers must be employees, severely constrain the policy options.

Once we begin to think outside those traditional givens, however, new possibilities appear that create an entirely new set of opportunities for policy action. Against the background of the problems with existing arrangements, the implications of teacher ownership stand out clearly, highlighting the potential to change significantly the following ongoing national discussions:

### Unblocking the Problem of "Getting to Scale" with the Improvement of Learning

Ownership has the potential to change practices at the core of education, not directly, at first, but as ownership creates incentives for teachers that do not exist today. An incentive is a reason to act combined with an opportunity to act. (Both are essential: a reason without the opportunity produces nothing; the opportunity without a reason produces nothing.) Ownership provides both the reason and the opportunity.

The analysis by Cuban, Elmore, and others assumes—realistically, given present arrangements—that teachers have little, if any, incentive to change their practices, and that intrinsic motivation is effective only with a limited number of teachers (Elmore, 1996; Cuban, 1984, 1990). And clearly—given present arrangements—there is nothing in it (financially) for the teachers, no real incentives for teachers to make the effort needed to adopt better practices in their own self-interest (Elmore, 1996). Most proposals for changing practice, as a result, look toward training, toward some form of new professional standards, and toward exhortation and pressure from peers.

Potentially, ownership is the alternative to the "existing flawed institutional arrangements and incentives structures" that Elmore calls for (1996). Ownership creates an incentive for teachers to change in their own interest; it creates a reason for them to act, and—because owners make the decisions—the opportunity for them to act, especially when pursued in a charter context.

Within this alternative institutional arrangement teachers have the freedom to adapt materials and methods to the differences among students, to individualize learning activity, and to modify the use of time in ways that allow students to pursue topics that interest them. There is an incentive, a reason combined with an opportunity, to do this. In addition, teacher owners will be inclined to respond to this incentive because the increased student success likely to result from these changes will further enhance their own professional (and perhaps also economic) rewards. (See chapter 6 for a discussion of the

EdVisions Cooperative where the TPP has done precisely what is described above.)

### Making Teachers the Leaders

Beyond simply providing teachers with the potential for leadership, ownership imposes the obligation of leadership. Teachers must become organizational leaders and professional leaders, and they must select and arrange the administrative leadership that serves them and their organization.

The idea of teacher leadership (teachers in charge of the learning) has the potential to eliminate the difficulty of trying to solve the problem of poor student learning by upgrading the supply and the skills of administrators, a tactic currently pursued by some schools and districts. (Any effort to strengthen leadership that omits entirely the role of teachers seems, on the face of it, absurd.)

Ownership would also bring into education the dual structure of leadership common in most professional organizations. This sort of structure exists in some medical partnerships, for example, with a chief doctor and an administrator, and in law firms, with a managing partner and an office administrator. In both cases, the administrators work for the professionals.

Ownership has the potential, too, to be a route for teachers to the control of professional issues that their unions have been trying—without notable success, given the resistance of boards of education—to win for them through bargaining. Among these are control over admission to practice; control of the standards of practice; control over the evaluation of practice and the program for the improvement of practice; control over the rewards (compensation) for practice; and the decision on the methods and materials to be used and on the work assignments. Teachers may, in fact, be able to get to professional status faster through ownership than through bargaining. In the district sector, with the current bureau arrangement, teacher control of professional issues may, in fact, restrict the potential for change. A contract arrangement, on the other hand, may increase the potential for change.

### Speeding Up Adoption of New Technologies

Owners invest in new and more productive technology because the rewards flow to them. Where the workers are not the owners, they often resist new technologies. But where the workers are the owners, a powerful incentive exists for the implementation of new and better methods that make the work both easier and more profitable. The idea of teacher ownership combines work and ownership in education and creates potential gains in productivity that can be captured by the teachers.

In an article in *The Economist*, June 28, 1984, Max Geldens, then a director of McKinsey & Company, ran the parallel with agriculture. On the American family farm, work and ownership were combined, and the implementation of technology, after about 1870 (new machinery, new seeds, new cropping practices), was dramatic. Farming became both easier and much more profitable. By contrast, in the factories, where work and ownership were divided and the gains from the new technologies accrued mainly to the owners, the workers had to organize and strike to win a share of the gains, and a long period of industrial strife ensued (Geldens, 1984).

To use the simplified evolution of the economy from farmer to worker to clerk, we are now in what people typically call an information economy. It is instructive to ask people which of the two earlier stages the new information economy seems more like. Most people, thinking of the way information activities have moved away from a factory setting, say the information economy is like farming. And clearly this is true: scale is reduced, and the capital requirements for information work are dramatically lower than for manufacturing. Surely the capital requirements for going into teaching must be far lower than the capital costs today of going into farming.

The question is inescapable: why, then, is education organized on the model of an old industrial corporation with the school district organized and run like an automobile factory, with its central office and its branch plants and its employee labor force? Even many industrial corporations have now moved away from this model of organization.

The implication—the potential—of the ownership model for teaching is for a dramatic improvement in productivity in this system of high labor costs. In the 1980s this potential was not present; the new ideas about teacher ownership and autonomous public schools had not yet been developed. Today both teachers and the technology industry can tap into that potential; the new technologies are simply waiting to be implemented.

This potential for productivity has big implications for the industry that makes and sells new learning technologies. In the K–12 education system, these firms have been marketing their equipment to superintendents, assuming that these managers can get their employees (teachers) to use it. The suppliers have not thought about teacher ownership; and they have not contemplated the effort at institutional change required to introduce the opportunity for teacher ownership. Twenty years ago when this was suggested to Bill Ridley, the executive in charge of creating and marketing education services at Control Data Corporation, he buried his face in his hands. "I haven't got time to talk to the teachers," he said (Kolderie, conversation with Ridley).

Today, with the progress already underway to create new arrangements in K–12 public education, the potential is ready to be realized. This is important. It would not be overstating the case to say that the large-scale introduction of information technology into education—more importantly, its continuing and developing *use* in the schools—depends on a restructuring of the idea of "school" to introduce the incentives, reasons, and opportunities that teacher ownership provides.

### Teacher Shortages

The ownership idea has the potential to attract good teachers into the profession—to attract the best people for the job. If teacher ownership has anticipated the other effects, it will make the work more rewarding professionally. In other words, ownership will attract better people by making teaching a better job.

Some teachers, at least, will be attracted by the opportunity to be in control and to be creative. Ownership will offer opportunities for growth that do not exist in the current employment arrangement. Finally, the incentive that ownership provides for an increase in productivity also contains some real prospect for better economic rewards, as teacher owners capture the gains from more efficient and effective work. Districts contracting with TPPs should have the opportunity, as well, to pay differentially by specialty area, offering more for teachers in areas of shortage, such as mathematics and science.

### Recasting Financial Issues

Ownership opens up a new dimension of economic, as well as professional, growth for teachers. It creates the potential for them to decrease the costs of existing operations and to keep, for use in the program or as personal income, whatever they do not need to spend. At the same time, it creates the potential for teacher groups to enlarge the scale of their operations, to serve more than one school or more than one district, and to increase their income from these new sources as well. In Minnesota there is also an opportunity to move into the market created in 1997 by the tax credit providing supplementary services to families buying after-school, evening, or summer education and training for their children.

Organizations owned by teachers will be organizations on contract to a school or to a district. They will exist as a business enterprise, rather than in a bureau model. The contract arrangement tends to increase the attention paid to objectives, results, educational performance, and financial performance. This creates accountability in the system. In an employment arrangement, one person or entity hires another, and both hope for the best. In a contract arrangement, the party who initiates the contract must be explicit about what the party providing contracted services must do, about how both parties will know whether, in fact, the work has been done to the satisfaction of the contracting party, and about what will happen if the work is not done satisfactorily. Strategically, a country interested in greater accountability—standards, measurement, and consequences—would immediately shift all its schools and learning programs to a contract arrangement.

In a professional partnership, teachers are obliged to make, themselves, the trade-offs between compensation and program that are made in the present district arrangement (or, often, *not* made) between contending parties, the board representing ownership and the union representing teachers. When internalized within the professional group, these decisions (and decisions on personnel) may have quite a different character.

As an example, we offer the experience of the teachers' organization serving Minnesota New Country School (see chapter 6). In November 1998, two newly elected board members of the district board sat in on the annual meeting of the school and its sponsor, LeSueur-Henderson School District. These new district board members were confused when they heard that the school ended its year with a surplus of about $80,000. (At that point, the LeSueur-Henderson School district still had not settled its contract with its teachers.) One of these new board members asked Brian Swenson, the chair of the board of Minnesota New Country School, "How is it possible to end the year with a surplus?" Swenson answered, "The board of the school doesn't have anything to do with teacher compensation. The teachers aren't the school's employees." This answer confused the new board members even more. So one of the teachers explained that these decisions are made inside the teacher group, EdVisions Cooperative. "We had to ask ourselves," this teacher said, "how we could tell the kids they weren't going to have an upgrade in their software next year because we wanted to take out more in salary for ourselves."

To people in the middle of the endless argument about money for schools, this is an amazing remark to hear from a teacher. However, the balancing of interests reflected in this teacher's remark is entirely logical for teachers working in an ownership and contract arrangement: if the TPP underpays teachers, it will not have any teachers, so it will not have a school. If the TPP overpays teachers and shortchanges the program, it will not have any students, so it will not have a school. As a result, teachers in the TPP make a trade-off, with integrity as the balancing factor among the divergent interests.

## Capturing the Potential of TPPs

As this brief sketch should indicate, the implications of the ownership model for teachers run to the heart of some of the most important issues and problems that policy leaders face in American public education—educational, professional, and financial.

Realizing these implications and capturing their potential will not be easy, but we should be optimistic. The problems blocking change have to be removed in the interests of our country and our children. The solutions cannot be found within the traditional regulated public utility model of district organization and within the traditional model of teacher employment. So, inevitably, policy leadership will find them outside these traditional givens.

Improvement is necessary, and things that are necessary tend to happen. Changes in a system do generate a new set of problems, of course, because a system is a collection of interacting parts. As the idea of teacher ownership develops into K–12 public education, the roles of boards and administrators and unions will change in response, as earlier sections in this chapter have made clear. And these secondary changes—these adjustments in the institution, in response to the growth of teacher ownership—will themselves have implications for policy and policymakers.

There is no space here, and really no need, to explore these adjustments and implications in detail. Their existence is not an argument against moving ahead with the change to ownership. And we can only guess at what they might be: everything will depend on what actually happens.

But it is fairly predictable that the growth of the TPP model will make it necessary for policy leadership to change a number of the provisions of law which now assume the bureau model—the district and its owned schools. As we have pointed out, retirement programs may need to be made portable; boards of education will need to know less about how to hire employees and to run organizations and more about how to be smart buyers; superintendents will have to adjust to this new role; job expectations for principals are certainly likely to change with the development of the partnership model for the organization of schools. These changes have implications for the education of administrators and boards: few education and training programs currently teach courses in how to "buy right." To the extent that teacher ownership appears initially in the charter sector of public education, laws may need to be adjusted to make it easier for teachers to have the same opportunity in the district sector as well.

Beyond this it is hard to see. Teachers unions may decide to resist the appearance of teacher ownership—but they may not. Unions are democratic organizations and their leadership will not readily oppose what the members want. Spending on K–12 education may grow more slowly—or it may not. If schools and learning improve, the public might be willing to spend more, realizing that, with a TPP, they get more.

# EDVISIONS COOPERATIVE

## An Example of a Teacher Professional Partnership

In September 1994, the Minnesota New Country School was created. The Le Sueur-Henderson School District sponsored the charter. In the past seven years the school has gained national attention and acclaim for being an economically successful school that has no courses, no classes, and no employees. Truly an example of redesign and reallocation, the school is a model of what school leaders can do to foster greater community and parent involvement, a market-driven approach and a new level of accountability for both teachers and students.

A group of individuals made up of a school board member, three teachers, and parents from Henderson and Le Sueur became interested in starting a charter school in 1992–1993 after the initial charter law was instituted in Minnesota. The innovative concept of allowing teachers and parents to start their own schools and then to accept greater accountability in exchange for this freedom appealed to this group.

After many meetings with teachers, parents, and community members, a proposal was presented to the Le Sueur-Henderson School District Board. The initial request was turned away. However, the district began strategic planning and realized it wanted more innovation and freedom of choice within the district education system. The proposal was brought to the board again, and it voted to sponsor Minnesota New Country School in the early winter of 1993.

The initial opening of the school was accomplished with no federal or state start-up funds. Two agencies provided grant money and technical assistance in the early stages: the Center for School Change of the Humphrey Institute of Public Affairs, University of Minnesota, under the direction of Joe Nathan; and Designs for Learning, under the leadership of Wayne Jennings. Both Nathan and Jennings were instrumental in starting the St. Paul Open School in the 1970s. With the $70,000 grant funds from the two organizations, the teacher advisors on the planning team developed methods and concepts about curriculum, developed a technology plan, and purchased computers, designed the renovation of buildings, marketed the school to students and parents, and did all the necessary legal paperwork.

One of the reasons the founders of Minnesota New Country School developed a teacher owner model was the absence of satisfying roles for teachers. They believed that teachers could create an atmosphere of ownership and fulfillment if they took complete control of the learning environment and responsibility for their own development. Daniel C. Mott, an attorney specializing in cooperative law, and Ted Kolderie of the Center for Policy Studies, suggested that the teachers form a workers' cooperative. A cooperative, they believed, would allow teachers working at the school the control they had been seeking. Thus, when the school was organized, a cooperative, with the teachers and other interested parties as members, was also formed. With a grant from the National Cooperative Bank Development Corporation and with Mott's help, the founders of the school put together the organization's bylaws. This teacher-owned cooperative, called EdVisions Cooperative, is the first and only workers' cooperative operating in the public school sector. As of August 2001, the EdVisions Cooperative has grown to eight schools and 120 members.

EdVisions Cooperative contracts separately with each of the eight charter school boards for learning services. The EdVisions Cooperative board of directors is made up of two persons elected by at-large members of EdVisions Cooperative plus two persons from each charter school, selected by their respective site teams. Although the board of directors has input into the processes for admitting new teachers into the cooperative, staff development, merit pay, and assessment, the teacher site team at the school manages the learning program and makes all personnel and financial decisions.

To better understand EdVisions Cooperative and its success we will provide a brief summary of Minnesota New Country School, the cooperative's first site, and then move on to a more complete discussion of where matters stand today.

## MINNESOTA NEW COUNTRY SCHOOL

### Overview

Minnesota New Country School, the first school served by EdVisions Cooperative, is an ungraded middle and high school with 110 students. The program is personalized, integrated, and project-based. Students develop independent learning skills as they complete process-based standards under the Minnesota State Profiles of Learning.

Students at Minnesota New Country School do not complete courses or classes. Students, in groups or individually, choose topics, plan, research, and complete academic study via hands-on projects that result in tangible, real-life products. The process is coached by teaching staff to engage students in studies that follow their interests, are closely related to experiences they will engage in when they complete formal school, include community experts whenever possible, and cover state inquiry-based standards. The school functions within an advisor/advisee system with a ratio of one advisor to seventeen students. Students are initially assigned to advisors but may choose different advisors each year. Some have stayed with the same advisor for the entire six years.

The teacher advisors act as generalists in helping their students achieve standards throughout the curriculum. A process of project proposals and project assessment has been developed by the teacher advisors, allowing for tracking of student accomplishment of knowledge, application, and process skills leading to independent learning skills.

The building space is utilized much differently than in a typical school. The students all have personal workstations with access to computers and other technology. The building has open spaces available for meetings and project development, as well as a media center, art room, shop, and break rooms. The ratio of one computer to every one-and-a-half students allows access to the Internet and various programs to all students.

Community projects are encouraged, with students developing businesses, doing internships, and utilizing community experts in their projects. Parents are involved to a great extent in the development of personalized learning plans for all students and have input into projects. All students present projects in demonstrations to the public at "presentation nights." Also, each senior must complete a major senior project and make a presentation to the public before graduation. The public has an opportunity to assess the presentations, giving real-world feedback and creating an expectation of real-world quality for the projects.

The primary purpose for the creation of the learning program at Minnesota New Country School was to address student interest in learning. By creating a program that allowed students choice, allowing for learning styles to be addressed, and by allowing access to technology in a student responsible format, student interest soared.

A secondary purpose was the access to computer-driven technology, which in the regular school setting was rarely available to students. By having computers available at all times, student interest and abilities to use various programs increased dramatically.

It was the mission of the school to develop a different type of student, one who would have skills to learn from the world, who would have the self-esteem and poise to interact positively with real-world problems. By fostering projects with community members and experts in various fields, Minnesota New Country School students develop the ability to deal with flexibility and ambiguity, unforeseen obstacles and opportunities, and have become skilled at working with both adults and other students.

The program at the Minnesota New Country School has resulted in satisfaction on the part of students and parents. Surveys show that 100 percent of the parents agree or strongly agree that their child likes school; 96 percent of parents agree or strongly agree that their student enjoys project-based learning; 94 percent of the students agree or strongly agree that the personalized learning program is important; and 99 percent of students agree or strongly agree they like learning through projects (*Minnesota New Country School Seventh Annual Report*, 2000). These are astounding numbers when compared with surveys of other local high schools.

Students have typically performed on par with or better than their counterparts on state-mandated reading, writing, and math tests. All students who have graduated in the past three years have passed the basic skills tests. College bound students' scores on ACT and SAT tests are in the normal range, and 66.7 percent have gone on to higher education. The school was the first to graduate students with the full number of Profiles of Learning requirements mandated by the Minnesota Legislature. Another verification of performance is the annual balances in the school budget that have produced surpluses and increased money to student programming and computers and allowed for teacher raises, making the salaries higher than average compared in the area (*Minnesota New Country School Seventh Annual Report*, 2000).

## Governance System

Teacher advisors in Minnesota New Country School have developed a truly teacher-owned, site-based management system. Overall responsibility for Minnesota New Country School is exercised by its charter school board. The learning program, however, is the responsibility of EdVisions Cooperative under a contract with the charter school board.

There is some overlap between the charter school board and the EdVisions Cooperative members who are teacher advisors at Minnesota New Country School. All charter schools in Minnesota, by law, must have a majority of licensed teachers on the charter school board. At the Minnesota New Country School, four teacher advisors and three parents make up the board. Parents of the students in attendance elect parents once a year, and teacher advisors are elected by their peers once a year.

Teachers having control of their learning program means they must take upon themselves an increasing number of roles. The school is under a flat management system. There are no administrators. For example, one of the teacher advisors does the administrative sign-off procedures for the state and federal documents. Another does the budgeting and finance reporting to the state, another does the state student reporting, and another is in charge of building and grounds and transportation. Extra stipends are paid to the teacher advisors for doing extra duties. Each teacher advisor is also on a number of committees, such as curriculum and assessment, finance, technology, personnel, and special education.

In addition, four of the teacher advisors serve on the charter school board, and two serve on the EdVisions Cooperative board of directors. In the 2000–2001 school year, the average teacher advisor was paid $42,500 before stipends for extra duties, which is similar to teachers with the same credentials in the independent school districts in the area.

Many regular school districts face difficulty in controlling and balancing revenues with expenditures. Because the budget is set and controlled by the teachers, and because so many services are supplied from within, Minnesota New Country School is able to operate on a budget in which only 60 percent of the budget goes to the teachers, yet the teachers have higher than average salaries. The school showed an ending balance of more than $168,000 in the fiscal year that ended on June 30, 2000.

As a result of having complete control of the budget process and the curriculum process, the staff at Minnesota New Country School is able to make changes in program very quickly. Because the staff is small enough to fit around one table, meets weekly and regularly, and also has informal communication, it is possible for the staff to agree on a change one day and institute changes the next day or next week. This flexibility creates an atmosphere of self-efficacy and control over one's own destiny, leading to more professionalism and, consequently, more fulfillment.

## EDVISIONS COOPERATIVE

As stated earlier, the founders of Minnesota New Country School also created EdVisions Cooperative, a teacher professional partnership, to address the need for a new arrangement in public education. The founders believed that a new model of educational entrepreneurship in the public system was necessary. Their purpose in organizing a teacher cooperative was to allow its members to be more accountable and responsible for the development and implementation of instructional programs. The organization of the cooperative was created as a viable alternative to the traditional top-down systems.

Ted Kolderie of the Center for Policy Studies in St. Paul encouraged the creation of the cooperative by asking the founders to consider this basic question: If teachers were not employees, what would they be? This led to a number of other questions pertaining to the present education arrangements. What if:

- Teachers were owners of their services rather than employees?
- Teachers were organized in small professional cooperatives rather than as employees of large districts?
- Teachers could have true site-based management and control of resources for education?
- Teachers' compensation was tied to school success, student performance, and professional development?

The teacher advisors at EdVisions Cooperative are member owners, not employees. They provide learning services and guarantee results through their contracts with Minnesota New Country School and seven other charter schools. The other schools (all in Minnesota) are River Bend Academy in Mankato, grades 7–12, sponsored by Minnesota Department of Children, Families, and Learning; El Colegio Charter School in Minneapolis, grades 9–12, sponsored by Augsburg College; Yankton Country School in Balaton, grades 9–12, sponsored by Yankton School Board; Hanska Community School in Hanska, grades K–8, sponsored by New Ulm School Board; Lafayette Charter School in Lafayette, grades K–8, sponsored by New Ulm School Board; Avalon Charter School in St. Paul, grades 9–12, sponsored by Hamline University; and Nerstrand Elementary School in Nerstrand, grades K–5, sponsored by Faribault School Board. The instructional programs are the responsibility of the cooperative members and program success depends upon the efforts of all educator members at each respective site.

Figure 6.1 shows the sponsorship and contractual relationships that constitute the EdVisions Cooperative environment. Le Sueur-Henderson School District is the sponsor of Minnesota New Country School. School Districts 2 and 3 are illustrative of the other school districts that sponsor separate charter schools, labeled Charter School A and Charter School B. Minnesota New Country School, Charter School A, Charter School B, and others not included on the chart independently enter into separate contracts with EdVisions Cooperative to provide the learning program for the charter school.

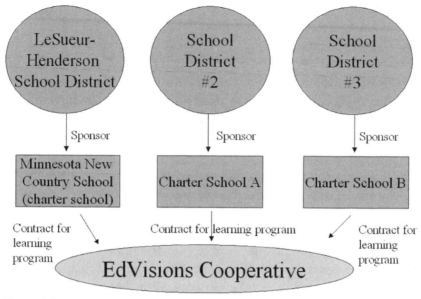

**Figure 6.1**

Figure 6.2 illustrates the fact that there are site teams, within EdVisions Cooperative, that are responsible for the learning program at their independent site. Each site team is responsible for carrying out the specific contract EdVisions Cooperative has entered into with their own charter school's board.

Having ownership in the learning programs requires that EdVisions Cooperative members take the necessary steps to be financially accountable; take care that students and parents are served according to their needs; and see to it that evaluation and assessment of their programs are undertaken with proper processes and reported to the sponsors, state, and community. Because the member owners are responsible for continually keeping the learning/instructional programs updated and viable, they must undertake a rigorous staff development program initiated by the cooperative membership.

Staff development plans, survey data from parents and students, and performance toward graduation standards are considered when determining the compensation or retention of each member. The cooperative sites do not have a tenure system. Each teacher advisor is contracted to a one-year, at-will contract. The cooperative supplies general ideas on

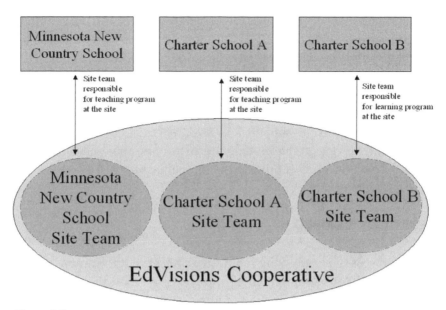

**Figure 6.2**

staff development and teacher advisor roles and responsibilities, but each local site team may create its own criteria and processes. Each site's management team is responsible for retaining and compensating staff based upon its self-developed criteria.

EdVisions Cooperative supplies some basic services to each of its member sites: payroll and benefits administration, staff development services, and help with evaluation and assessment of programs. As a result of the Gates-EdVisions Project, wherein the cooperative is charged with developing fifteen more high schools based upon the Minnesota New Country School model that will also result in ten more teacher ownership models similar to the cooperative. Recognizing that it may need to evolve as new schools seek membership, EdVisions Cooperative is contemplating the creation of local geographically linked cooperatives of charter schools. EdVisions would then become a discrete organization that operates as a service cooperative to provide better member benefits. As a service cooperative, it would provide service and procurement functions in order to supply common outsourcing needs to the cooperative members and be a marketing agent for members' supplying staff development within the cooperative and to independent districts.

The true benefit of the new arrangement created by the teachers' co-operative is just being felt in the educational establishment. There is an enormous interest on the part of educators, board members, and citizens across the country in the possibility of rearranging the current employer–employee labor relationship. Because of EdVisions Cooperative with its peer-review-led compensation, staff development tied to performance, as well as the support for entrepreneurial endeavors that the cooperative provides, educational enterprises are being challenged to re-think how education is provided to the public sector.

## LESSONS LEARNED

In the process of creating the innovative project-based learning model at Minnesota New Country School and creating a TPP, the founders of EdVisions Cooperative learned a number of lessons that may be of use to other educators considering the creation of such organizations. First and foremost is the change in mindset necessary for teachers to think of themselves as leaders and owners of their own enterprise and being strictly accountable for results. Teachers, especially in large systems, don't think of themselves as being responsible for the effectiveness of the entire organization. A TPP makes it impossible for teachers to ignore the operation and success of the school as a whole.

The employee–employer arrangement creates a mentality of us-against-them, rather than the mutual sense that we-are-in-this-together. As cooperative member owners, each individual must believe that the success of the whole is as important as the success of one; indeed, it is necessary to have overall success in order for a charter school to continue. The first lesson learned by EdVisions Cooperative personnel is that it is very difficult for teachers to think outside the employee paradigm. There seems to be an attitude, on the part of new members especially, that there will be automatic raises and lane changes without the necessary work invested in improving the program.

Some new members in EdVisions Cooperative sites also did not see the cooperative as anything other than an outside payroll provider. To many, the cooperative was transparent, an entity that could just as well not exist. For those who took an active part in building the cooperative and took advantage of its services, there was immediate ownership and viability. Investiture in the enterprise is high on the part of some and low on the part of others. Those who participated at a low level, however, still expected services to be of high quality. This led some members of the school sites active in the cooperative to take on more than their fair share of duties, while others were not involved at all.

The lesson in this is simple: obtain buy-in to the TPP before personnel decisions at a site are finalized. New members should receive in-service training about the level of participation needed for a viable enterprise to succeed and about what services are supplied by the TPP. The recommendation of EdVisions Cooperative is for the TPP to invite new members based upon established criteria for all sites, as the Edison Project does. Then the proper mindset can be created from the start and the need for in-service will be less.

Lesson number one leads to lesson number two: the need for new and different teacher preparation processes. Teacher candidates out of general college or university programs are not trained to think as entrepreneurs or risk-takers. Either the TPP will have to undertake a staff development process that leads to educators practicing as desired, or there needs to be pressure on lawmakers and policymakers to develop new alternative licensure programs. EdVisions Cooperative leadership recommends that TPP leaders become involved with colleges or universities, perhaps by an agreement or contract, to undertake a clinical program that will help align mindsets with the practices necessary to become teacher leaders and owners. Minnesota New Country School has entered into such an agreement with Minnesota State University–Mankato, under the auspices of the Center for School Change, with a grant from Cargill. In the 2000–2001 school year, New Country School hosted eight student teachers, one of whom was invited to become a teacher advisor for the 2001–2002 school year.

Alternative licensure programs at some colleges and universities may be more amenable to producing the type of teacher needed in a TPP, for example, master's of arts in teaching programs make it possible for persons with bachelor's degrees outside of the field of education to be retrained as teachers. These programs bring in people who have spent time in the workforce and have had experiences outside of classrooms in the real world. People with such experiences may be more open to becoming owners rather than laborers in the field of education.

The other alternative is to reform already existing programs by adding courses or experiences in economics or finance, adding administrative coursework and experience, or adding various clinical experiences that give novice teachers an opportunity to learn about what governance and leadership of a school involves. Adding courses to an already crowded docket of credits in education and other major coursework is problematic. Adding new alternative licensure programs may be more possible. EdVisions Cooperative is willing and able to enter into an agreement with a college or university to undertake an alternative licensure program, but the accomplishment of such a task is far into the future.

Lesson number three is linked to the above: the necessity of preparing teachers to become advisors of independent learning rather than providers of information. The major problem is to help students understand that they—not the teacher or the school—are responsible for their own learning. The most difficult thing for teachers trained in the traditional behaviorist lesson planning mode is to give up their sovereignty and their rigidity about the process and to train students in the process of becoming independent learners. This takes time and patience. Dee Grover Thomas, a teacher advisor at Minnesota New Country School, says: "You have to make the kids responsible. Don't do everything for them. Allow them to fail. Have patience they will become intrinsically motivated through their own interests" (as cited in Newell, 2001). Without patience, the tendency is to revert to old teaching habits.

Also necessary is a change in mindset from a belief in "learning content" to "learning process." Traditional teachers are prepared to divulge tidbits of information in doses, test on retention of the tidbits, and perceive this as learning. Grover Thomas explains it this way: "We have to make the shift from content to process. As information doubles every few years, it takes a great deal of arrogance to assume we can give them the information they need for a future we cannot see. They need to have a good process of learning what they need when that future arrives" (Newell, 2001). To support personalized, project-based, and integrated education methods, a constructivist, process-oriented mindset must be accepted by those who teach/advise. This has also proven to take some staff development time.

The fourth lesson learned by the founders of EdVisions Cooperative is that there is a great need to develop a process for good communication within the sites and the TPP. If the TPP does not wish to become another central office like the ones in many large school districts, it must develop a means by which teacher owners participate in decision making, and it must have ways in which changes can be made quickly and efficiently. Having all teacher advisors be part of committees and boards, with a clear line of communication among them, will alleviate the feeling of alienation. Providing staff development in open communication processes, such as the model of Restorative Justice Circles, may be of great benefit. The intent of the EdVisions Cooperative is to create a democratic process in which every individual's opinions and feelings matter—listening to all voices is mandatory. The cooperative idea is a democratic one. Processes had to be implemented to allow for all members to feel as if they were truly owners and contributing members. Creating these processes took time and training, but it was necessary.

The fifth lesson learned by the EdVisions Cooperative membership is the need for creation of a free flow of support, service, and technical assistance. If many sites are to be involved with the TPP, then all sites need to be connected via a network maintained by some staff persons. The organization cannot function well if all support personnel are also actively engaged in teaching and managing the school. The TPP must make it possible for staff development and technical assistance personnel to be free to actively engage in development work. It is useful if grants are available. However, at some point, the organization will have to assess the assistance available at each site and develop a support group or team. This time and support must be built into budgets.

EdVisions Cooperative also learned that it is impossible to carry on the work of being a teacher owner if teachers are not willing to commit to a great deal of work. With the freedom of controlling one's own destiny comes the responsibility that all business owners have: it is not an eight-to-four job. If things need to be taken care of, then it is necessary to put in extra time. With freedom comes accountability. This is especially true in a charter school. As Grover Thomas says, "Taking ownership means you can't sit back and think it is someone else's problem. Every problem is your problem. It takes a total commitment" (Newell, 2001). Unless all teacher advisors recognize this, the work of managing a school or groups of schools will fall to a few members, burning them out.

One of the most important lessons learned is that the work is worth the effort. Most teacher advisors feel the extra responsibility and accountability give them a greater sense of control and, consequently, a greater degree of satisfaction. Although some licensed staff went from this environment back to traditional teaching, most teacher advisors would not go back to being employees. The greater satisfaction of seeing students achieve, parents respond with satisfaction, and one's *own* school succeed leads to an overwhelming feeling of accomplishment.

## THE FUTURE

Verification of the effectiveness of the learning and governance programs of Minnesota New Country School and EdVisions Cooperative comes from the interest on the part of educators from across the nation and from the world. Hundreds of visitors have come from many states and foreign countries to visit and see how the programs work. Additionally, the school and the cooperative were awarded two dissemination grants in 2001. One of these grants, from federal start-up funds distributed through the State of Minnesota's Department of Children, Families, and Learning, was to disseminate information about Minnesota New Country School. This grant led to the opening of three schools. The second grant of $4.4 million from the Bill and Melinda Gates Foundation is for the creation of fifteen schools with the Minnesota New Country School learning model, which will also result in ten more teacher professional partnerships over a five-year period.

The future for teacher professional partnerships is wide open. Movements for changing the paradigm of the education establishment are growing everywhere. The time for creating new entities that will develop new approaches to education services has rapidly come upon us.

# CHANGING THE
# NATIONAL DISCUSSION

Some time in the 1980s, when the idea of teacher partnerships was around in its earlier form, a friend of ours tried it out one day at breakfast in Washington, D.C., with Albert Shanker, then president of the American Federation of Teachers.

Shanker listened. Then he was quiet a while. Then he said, "That's a totally new idea to me (Kolderie, 1988)."

## INITIATING A NATIONAL DISCUSSION OF
## TEACHER OWNERSHIP

It is a challenge to get a discussion started about a totally new idea. Here at the end of this guide—since one of the authors' objectives is in fact to begin a national discussion about the idea of teacher ownership—we should say a bit about the challenge of raising and discussing a "totally new idea." A few things seem obvious, but may be worth saying nevertheless.

*Point out that many new ideas that were in fact quickly adopted were met with skepticism when first presented.*

"Who the hell wants to hear actors talk?" a Hollywood studio executive asked when the idea of "talking pictures" first appeared.

The head of International Business Machines initially thought there might be a market for as many as twelve of these new things called computers.

"If God had intended us to fly he would have given us wings."

It's important to remember that the test is not whether the idea is new. It's whether the idea has merit.

### Urge people to start with the problems in education that teacher ownership might solve.

There's always a tendency in discussions about something new for people to resist at first. It's easy to feel things must be okay now—if we live with the current situation every day, things can't be too bad. And, as some British conservatives like to say: When it is not essential to change, it is essential not to change. Change is a risk. Why take the risk?

The burden is thrown, then, on the new idea to prove that it is not a risk at all, that if it is introduced it would work perfectly and have no negative side effects. If this can't be shown, then the new idea cannot be introduced.

We need to start at a different point, with a realistic understanding that things are far from perfect now. Then the new idea comes up in a different light.

As the chapter 5 section, "What Are the Implications" explains, public education faces a set of real and urgent problems for which policymakers do not at the moment have very good answers.

If we start with the understanding that some change is imperative, then all the ideas—including this one—can be discussed on the reasonable assumption that the test is to demonstrate not perfection, but simply a reasonable prospect that, on balance, if introduced, it would produce an improvement over the situation we have at the moment. The lifeboat isn't all that comfortable, but it's better than going down with the ship.

Emphasize that getting the discussion to have a great deal of intensity will require having a larger number of success stories.

If nothing happens except that people talk about it, the discussion of the new idea is likely to be theoretical and ideological. This is not very practical. It makes a lot more sense to get more working tests of the idea, and then to discuss it in terms of the various ways that it actually works.

And don't expect a lot of people to want to do this right at the start. Look at the birds on the telephone wire. Usually one bird leaves first. Others follow. If you find the idea attractive, start a teacher professional partnership or encourage someone else to do so.

### Watch out for the false arguments that "it can't be done" because there is no law or decisionmaking body specifically authorizing it.

The argument that teacher ownership can't be tried because it hasn't been specifically authorized is unworthy. No brand new idea has ever been specifically authorized: Things are never authorized before they're contemplated. Start with the assumption that, never having been contemplated, the idea certainly isn't specifically forbidden.

Arguments of this sort often come from people who simply don't like the new idea—whatever it may be—and want to deter you from trying it.

### Similarly, don't be deterred by questions of scalability.

One of the most common efforts to deflect a new idea is to say it's too small to bother with. Opponents will often say: "You want to do something significant. This is not significant. The big needs and the big opportunities are in the existing organizations. That's where you want to work. Be practical: Don't waste your time on things too small to make a difference."

Of course, until an idea has been tried, no one knows how "scalable" it may be. Some new ideas turn out not to have potential. But sometimes very large things do grow from what was at the start a very small beginning. It is good not to be disrespectful of small beginnings.

Urge people, too, to think in terms of the idea being scalable, replicable. Too much of this discussion today is about whether the new idea can itself grow large. Investment capital firms like to think this way. But often—especially in the early stages—the idea spreads faster than individual organizations grow. The big organizations come later . . . as a moment's reflection about the early history of the automobile or the airplane makes clear.

*Urge people to look at their local charter sector first.*

As earlier chapters explain, the teacher partnership idea can apply to a whole school, to a department of a school, or to a multischool program in a district. But the idea has first appeared in the new sector of public education created by the charter laws (see chapter 6).

These now exist in "live" form—meaning schools can and do actually get created—in perhaps twenty-five states. Innovations come a little easier in the charter sector, especially an innovation like teacher ownership. So it would make some sense to discuss this idea initially with persons there.

And, of course, discuss it when people are just beginning to think about the design of a new school and before they have moved to employ teachers in the conventional way. Explain the ownership idea to them; suggest they put the idea in front of the individuals they'd like to have come in as teachers as an option to think about that's available if the teachers wish.

*Don't confine efforts to the charter sector, though.*

Do talk also with teachers in the district sector. Think about the mathematics department or one of the science departments or the world language department of a big high school.

And for this purpose go to the disciplinary organizations: your state's association of teachers of science, your state's association of teachers of mathematics.

*Help people recognize that the idea will, and must, evolve.*

As the discussion gets started—and especially as the idea begins to be tried in more settings—the idea itself will evolve.

This happened almost immediately as the idea spread into Wisconsin from EdVisions Cooperative in Minnesota, where it started.

Wisconsin's charter law differs from Minnesota's: If teachers want to remain in the state retirement program in Wisconsin, they need to remain legally employees of the district.

This became a problem for one veteran Milwaukee teacher in a group that wanted to form a teacher cooperative (partnership). As it happened, her father had been a longtime union official. He went to work on her problem with a lawyer he'd known. They came up with a variation on the model that offers teachers a combination of employment for their economic life and ownership for their professional life (see appendix D).

It's amazing how people set on reaching a goal—in this case, owning their work—find creative ways to work around obstacles.

And in all these efforts at institutional innovation, it's probably good not to insist that all trials hold the idea to its original form. People will want to vary the idea to fit to what they see as their local situation, and that's probably okay.

*Show people how to be in touch with the national discussion and with efforts to try the ownership idea elsewhere.*

Internet technology is ideal for organizing a discussion and keeping abreast of existing and new teachers partnerships.

In the near future, you ought to be able to search for references to "teacher partnerships" and to "teacher ownership." The project that has produced this book will have a web site of its own, and there will be links on other web sites, such as www.charterfriends.org. The teacher cooperative at Henderson, Minnesota, has had its own web site for some time, and you can follow its progress at www.edvisions.com.

Encourage those interested in teacher ownership to develop e-mail networks, linking those exploring the idea and trying out one version or another.

## FINAL THOUGHTS

There is, of course, much discussion now about teachers and teaching in the national discourse about education. The articles and TV programs are forever asking: "How do we change teaching practice?" "How do we find enough good teachers?" "How do we strengthen school leadership?"

At the moment, this discussion is locked into the traditional assumption of employment: that teachers are employees; workers told what to do by their employers.

Most people accept this employee framework without even being conscious of it. The first step in a new national discussion is to identify this assumption. The next step is to challenge it. People need first to see that most professionals do not have to be employees, then to see that this opportunity to own their work can be extended to teachers as well. The discussion can then move to the what, the why, and the how of opening up the professional partnership model for teachers. We hope that in this latter discussion this guide will prove to be a help, a resource.

# APPENDIX A

## Comparison of Legal Structures for Doing Business as a Teacher Professional Organization*

A.  Selecting a structure

There are a number of organizational structures that may be available to teachers forming a professional organization. Each alternative structure will provide certain advantages and disadvantages relative to the other alternatives. The ultimate decision on the structure of the entity is often complex and may vary from group to group, depending on the specific objective of that group. Teachers contemplating the formation of a professional organization should obtain competent legal advice to assist in evaluating the organizational structure that will best help them meet their objectives.

B.  Definitions

The various organizational options available to teacher professional organizations include:

1.  C-Corporations: C-corporations are traditional business corporations organized under state corporate laws and taxed under Subchapter C of the Internal Revenue Code.

2.  S-Corporations: S-corporations are traditional business corporations organized under state corporate laws and taxed under Subchapter S of the Internal Revenue Code.

*Source: Daniel C. Mott.

3. Cooperatives: Cooperatives are incorporated under state co-operative laws and operate on a "cooperative basis." Cooperatives are taxed under Subchapter T of the Internal Revenue Code.

4. General Partnerships: General partnerships (GPs) are formed by contract and are governed by state partnership law. GPs are not separate tax-paying entities for tax law purposes. The income and losses of the partnership are "passed through" to the partners.

5. Limited Liability Partnerships: Limited liability partnerships (LLPs) are general partnerships that have elected to limit the liability of the partners by complying with specific state law requirements. LLPs are taxed under partnership rules. LLPs will be combined with GPs for purposes of this outline.

6. Limited Liability Companies: Limited liability companies (LLCs) are incorporated under state LLC law. LLCs have characteristics of both corporations and partnerships. LLCs are taxed under partnership tax rules.

7. Nonprofit Corporations: Nonprofit corporations are incorporated under state nonprofit corporation laws. Nonprofit corporations may not make distributions of income to their members. Nonprofit corporations are taxed under subchapter C of the Internal Revenue Code. Nonprofit corporations may apply for a tax exemption under Section 501(c) of the Internal Revenue Code. However, this outline assumes that tax exempt status will not be available to a teacher professional organization, and the exemption is not specifically addressed.

8. Limited Partnerships: Limited partnerships (LPs) are organized under state limited partnership laws. LPs typically have one or more general partners and a number of limited partners. General partners have joint and several liability for the obligations of the LP. The liability of limited partners is limited to their capital investment. The LP is an unlikely structure for a teacher professional organization and is not specifically addressed in this outline.

C. Legal characteristics

Key legal characteristics include ownership, duration, liability exposure, transferability of interests, and management responsibility. There will be, however, additional legal characteristics that should be considered in comparing the various entities under any given circumstances.

1. Ownership

   a. C-Corporations: No limit on number of owners; no restrictions on eligibility of owners; unlimited classes of stock or other securities.

   b. S-Corporations: seventy-five shareholder limit; LLCs, partnerships, nonresident aliens, and certain estates and trusts are not eligible owners; only one class of stock permitted, but voting differences allowed (these are tax, rather than legal, requirements).

   c. Cooperatives: No limit on number of members; usually there are restrictions on eligibility of members (e.g., limited to teachers); unlimited classes of stock or other forms of equity; generally, voting is on a one member one vote basis.

   d. Partnerships: No limit on maximum number of partners; no restrictions on eligibility of partners.

   e. LLCs: No limit on maximum number of members; no restrictions on eligibility of members; unlimited classes of membership interests.

   f. Nonprofit Corporations: No limit on maximum number of members; no restrictions on eligibility of members; unlimited classes of membership.

2. Duration

   a. C-Corporations: Perpetual existence, unless limited in the articles of incorporation.

   b. S-Corporations: Perpetual existence, unless limited in the articles of incorporation.

   c. Cooperatives: Perpetual existence, unless limited in the articles of incorporation.

   d. Partnerships: A general partnership or limited liability partnership is terminated (1) by agreement of the partners; (2)

on a partner's death, bankruptcy, dissolution, or other disaffiliation, unless the partners agree to continue the partnership; or (3) by court order.

e. LLCs: An LLC is terminated (1) by expiration of the period
of duration provided in the articles of organization; (2) by
agreement of the members; (3) on a member's death, bankruptcy, dissolution, or other disaffiliation, unless the remaining members unanimously agree to avoid dissolution, unless
the articles of organization or member control agreement
provide for consent by fewer than all of the members or for
a separate right to continue; or (4) by judicial dissolution.

f. Nonprofit Corporations: Perpetual existence unless limited
in the articles of incorporation.  ·

3. Liability exposure

a. C-Corporations: A shareholder is liable only for the shareholder's capital contribution. In some limited circumstances, the courts may "pierce the corporate veil" and find
the shareholder personally liable.

b. S-Corporations: A shareholder is liable only for the shareholder's capital contribution. In some limited circumstances, the courts may "pierce the corporate veil" and
find the shareholder personally liable.

c. Cooperatives: A member is liable only for the member's
capital contribution.

d. Partnerships: All general partners are jointly and severally
liable for the debts of the partnership.

e. LLCs: A member of an LLC is liable only for the member's capital contribution. In some limited circumstances,
the courts may "pierce the corporate veil" and find the
member personally liable.

f. Nonprofit Corporations: Members typically make no capital contribution. Members are not personally liable for the
obligations of the corporation.

4. Transferability of interests

a. C-Corporations: An interest in a C-corporation is readily
and easily marketable by a transfer of stock certificate unless restricted by the shareholders.

b. S-Corporations: An interest in an S-corporation is readily and easily marketable by a transfer of stock certificate unless restricted by the shareholders.

c. Cooperatives: Shares of stock or a membership in a cooperative are transferable only with the consent of the board of directors.

d. Partnerships: The addition of a new partner or the transfer of a general partner's governance interest often requires consent of other partners.

e. LLCs: Financial rights are freely transferable, unless otherwise agreed upon by the members. Governance rights typically are not transferred to a nonmember without the consent of all the other members.

f. Nonprofit Corporations: Membership in a nonprofit corporation is typically not transferable. Membership arises as a result of status, not capital investment.

5. Governance responsibility

a. C-Corporations: Governance of a C-corporation is by a board of directors elected by the voting shareholders.

b. S-Corporations: Governance of an S-corporation is by a board of directors elected by the voting shareholders.

c. Cooperatives: Governance of a cooperative is by a board of directors elected by the voting members.

d. Partnerships: Unless the partnership agreement provides otherwise, all general partners participate in governance and share that responsibility jointly.

e. LLCs: Governance of an LLC is by a board of governors elected by the voting members, subject to the provisions of a member control agreement.

f. Nonprofit Corporations: Governance of a nonprofit corporation is by a board of directors elected by the voting members.

D. Tax characteristics

Key tax characteristics include treatment of income and losses, distributions, liquidation of the business, and sale of an ownership interest. There will be, however, additional tax characteristics that should be considered in comparing the various entities under any given circumstances.

1. Treatment of income and losses
    a. C-Corporations: All corporate income is taxed at the corporate level and again at the shareholder level when distributed as dividends; losses are deductible only by the corporation when it has offsetting income (fifteen-year carryover).
    b. S-Corporations: Corporate income determined at entity level and liability to pay the tax is passed through to shareholders regardless of whether distributed; allocations made on a per-share basis; losses pass through to shareholders and are deductible to the extent of basis, subject to at-risk rules and passive loss limitations.
    c. Cooperatives: Any net income in excess of dividends and additions to capital reserves is distributed on the basis of patronage; generally, cooperatives may avoid federal income tax on patronage-sourced earnings if income is allocated to patrons in the prescribed manner; normally patrons/members must include in income the amount of any patronage dividend that is paid in money, a qualified written notice of allocation or other property received from the cooperative during the taxable year; losses are generally deductible only at the cooperative level.
    d. Partnerships/LLCs: Income determined at entity level and liability to pay the tax is passed through to partners/members regardless of whether distributed; special allocations permitted; losses pass through to partners/members and are deductible to the extent of basis, subject to at-risk rules and passive loss limitations (indefinite carryover).
    e. Nonprofit Corporations: Any taxable income is retained and is taxed at the corporate level. The corporation may not distribute income to the members.
2. Distributions
    a. C-Corporations: Distributions of cash taxed as ordinary income to the extent of earnings and profits.
    b. S-Corporations: Distributions of cash taxed to the extent they exceed a shareholder's basis in stock.

    c. Cooperatives: Patronage dividends may be distributed as cash, capital stock credits, allocated patronage equities, revolving fund certificates, or other written evidence of allocation; the cooperative receives a patronage dividend deduction while patrons must take patronage dividends into income in the year received.

    d. Partnerships/LLCs: Distributions of cash taxed to the extent they exceed a partner/member's basis in partnership/LLC interest.

    e. Nonprofit Corporation: Distributions to members are not permitted.

  3. State tax issues

    The foregoing tax discussion focused on federal taxation issues. State and local taxation, however, will be an important consideration in selecting the appropriate entity. Most states follow the federal income tax classification of LLCs as either partnerships or corporations. Some states, however, treat all LLCs as partnerships and a few tax all LLCs as corporations or impose a franchise tax on LLCs.

E. Other considerations

  In addition to the customary legal and tax considerations outlined above, there are a number of other factors that are relevant to consider in the context of a teacher professional organization.

  1. Public relations

    a. Corporations, Limited Liability Companies, and Partnerships: These structures are typically associated with for-profit activities. In the context of public education, the for-profit motive may be viewed negatively.

    b. Cooperatives: Although cooperatives often have a profit or entrepreneurial motivation, they are often viewed as having a positive public purpose. This may provide a public relations advantage.

    c. Nonprofit Corporations: There would likely be no negative public relations from a public perspective. Potential members may question the structure.

2. Political considerations

In selecting a structure for a teacher professional organization, consideration should be given to the implication of the structure for public policy purposes. To the extent that public funding is ultimately paying the teachers, politicians must be comfortable with the structure. The public relations considerations outlined above will also be relevant when considering the political consequences of a particular structure.

# APPENDIX B

## Options for Private Retirement Plans for Teacher Professional Partnerships

There are six private retirement plans available to organizations such as TPPs. Each of these options is a qualified retirement plan:

- SER-IRA
- Simple IRA
- Simple 401(k)
- Safe Harbor 401(k)
- 401(k) not Safe Harbor
- Money Purchase Pension Plan

The following questions provide an overview of the differences among these options:

1. What are the limits on the number of individuals who may participate in a plan?
2. What are the eligibility requirements for individuals?
3. What employer contributions are possible and/or required?
4. Are there any limits on the maximum amount an employer may contribute?

5. Are there any limits on the maximum amount that can be contributed to an individual account?
6. What are the pretax deferral rules?
7. What are the deadlines for set-up and contributions?
8. What are the reporting requirements?

TPPs should seek competent and appropriate advice and counsel when considering these options.

# RETIREMENT PLAN OPTIONS

| TYPE OF PLAN | SEP-IRA | SIMPLE IRA | SIMPLE 401(k) PLAN | SAFE HARBOR 401(k) PLAN | 401(k) PLAN NOT SAFE HARBOR | MONEY PURCHASE PENSION PLAN |
|---|---|---|---|---|---|---|
| **Size Limit** | • No limit | • 100 members or less | • 100 members or less | • No limit | • No limit | • No limit |
| **Eligibility**<br><br>Note: Plan sponsors can always choose to make eligibility requirements less stringent. The limitations shown here are the most restrictive under ERISA guidelines. | Members must be allowed to participate if:<br>• Age 21 or older<br>• Employed in three of preceding five years | Members must be allowed to participate if:<br>• Earned $5,000 in any two preceding years and expected to in current year | Plan can exclude:<br>• Members under age 21 and<br>• Members with less than one year of service<br><br>The employer can exclude other groups as long as certain coverage tests are passed. The exclusions cannot be based on age (other than as noted above) or compensation. | Plan can exclude:<br>• Members under age 21 and<br>• Members with less than one year of service<br><br>The employer can exclude other groups as long as certain coverage tests are passed. The exclusions cannot be based on age (other than as noted above) or compensation. | Plan can exclude:<br>• Members under age 21 and<br>• Members with less than one year of service<br><br>The employer can exclude other groups as long as certain coverage tests are passed. The exclusions cannot be based on age (other than as noted above) or compensation. | Plan can exclude:<br>• Members under age 21 and<br>• Members with less than one year of service<br><br>The employer can exclude other groups as long as certain coverage tests are passed. The exclusions cannot be based on age (other than as noted above) or compensation. |
| **Employer Contributions**<br><br>Note: Maximum eligible compensation is limited to $170,000 per member in 2001. | Only employer contributions are allowed<br><br>Employer contributions are not required in every plan year | Required employer contributions are:<br>• 100% match up to 3% of compensation (can be reduced to 1% in two of five years)<br>or<br>• 2% of all eligible compensation | Required employer contributions are:<br>• 100% match up to 3% of compensation<br>or<br>• 2% of all eligible compensation<br>• If the plan is top heavy, a 3% annual employer contribution may be required | Required annual employer contributions are:<br>• 100% match up to 3% of compensation and 50% of 3 – 5% of compensation<br>or<br>• At least 3% all eligible compensation<br>• If the plan is top heavy, a 3% annual employer contribution may be required | • If the plan is top heavy, a 3% annual employer contribution may be required<br>• Employer contributions may be specified in the plan document or may be determined annually at the discretion of the employer | • Annual employer contribution level (of 1 – 25% of compensation) must be specified in the plan document<br>• Annual employer contributions are required<br>• If the plan is top heavy, a 3% annual employer contribution may be required |
| **Maximum Annual Employer Contributions** | 15% of each eligible member's compensation | 15% of each eligible member's compensation | 15% of total eligible compensation. This limit is applied at the plan level | 15% of total eligible compensation. This limit is applied at the plan level | 15% of total eligible compensation. This limit is applied at the plan level | 25% of total eligible compensation. This limit is applied at the plan level |

# RETIREMENT PLAN OPTIONS

| TYPE OF PLAN | SEP-IRA | SIMPLE IRA | SIMPLE 401(k) PLAN | SAFE HARBOR 401(k) PLAN | 401(k) PLAN NOT SAFE HARBOR | MONEY PURCHASE PENSION PLAN |
|---|---|---|---|---|---|---|
| Maximum Annual Contributions to Each Member's Account (2001 limits) | 15% of compensation | 15% of compensation | Lesser of 25% of eligible compensation or $35,000 | Lesser of 25% of eligible compensation or $35,000 | Lesser of 25% of eligible compensation or $35,000 | Lesser of 25% of eligible compensation or $35,000 |
| Pretax Deferral Limits (2001) | N/A—No pretax deferrals allowed | $6,500 | $6,500 | $10,500 | $10,500 | N/A—No pretax deferrals allowed |
| Vesting of Employer Contributions | Contributions must be 100% vested immediately | Vesting can be 100% immediate. A vesting schedule may be implemented, but in no case can it be longer than a seven-year graded schedule | Vesting can be 100% immediate. A vesting schedule may be implemented, but in no case can it be longer than a seven-year graded schedule | Contributions must be 100% vested immediately | Vesting can be 100% immediate. A vesting schedule may be implemented, but in no case can it be longer than a seven-year graded schedule | Vesting can be 100% immediate. A vesting schedule may be implemented, but in no case can it be longer than a seven-year graded schedule |
| Deadline for Set-Up/ Contributions | • Set-up and contribute by employer's tax filing deadline, plus extension for prior year contribution | • Plan must be adopted by October 1 of current year <br>• 60-day notice to all eligible members <br>• Employer contributions must be made by business' tax filing deadline, plus extensions <br>• Member contributions must be deposited as soon as possible; not to exceed 30 days after month withheld | • Must be adopted by December 31 (or last day of tax year) <br>• Employer contributions must be made by business' tax filing deadline, plus extensions <br>• Member contributions must be deposited as soon as possible; not to exceed 15 days after month withheld | • Must be adopted by December 31 (or last day of tax year) <br>• Employer contributions must be made by business' tax filing deadline, plus extensions <br>• Member contributions must be deposited as soon as possible; not to exceed 15 days after month withheld | • Must be adopted by December 31 (or last day of tax year) <br>• Employer contributions must be made by business' tax filing deadline, plus extensions <br>• Member contributions must be deposited as soon as possible; not to exceed 15 days after month withheld | • Must be adopted by December 31 (or last day of tax year) <br>• Employer contributions must be made by business' tax filing deadline, plus extensions |
| Annual Form 5500* Reporting Requirements | • Form 5500 is NOT required | • Form 5500 is NOT required | • Form 5500 must be filed annually | • Form 5500 must be filed annually | • Form 5500 must be filed annually | • Form 5500 must be filed annually |

* Form 5500 is the annual information return that is filed with the Department of Labor. For plan with over 100 eligible members, this filing also requires that an independent accounting firm audit the plan.

Source: *Larson, Allen, Weishair & Co., LLP.*

# APPENDIX C

## Outline of a Business Plan for a Teacher Professional Partnership

The following is an outline of potential topics to include in the business plan of a start-up TPP. Each plan will be different. Please note that plans for a TPP that has been operational for several years may be different as well.

At first glance, the outline may seem overwhelming to those not accustomed to putting together these types of plans. All of the topics included here are vital for inclusion in a start-up plan. An expert facilitator, experienced in developing business plans for start-up businesses, will be helpful in identifying what is needed.

   I. Executive summary
  II. The teacher professional partnership (TPP)
     (What does it want to do? How will it be structured, and how will it operate?)
     A. Vision—mission—values (guiding principles)
     B. Legal structure
     C. Governance/bylaw major provisions
     D. Leadership and administrative positions
        1. Skills and experience needed
        2. Accountability
        3. Who it will be?

    E. TPP membership
1. Admission requirements
2. Admission process
3. Provision for partners leaving the partnership
4. Capital requirements
    F. Standards of partnership
1. Performance measurement and improvement
2. Peer review
3. Professional development
4. Discipline
    G. Compensation (including fringe benefits)
    H. Sources of revenue
    I. Fees to be charged for teaching, consulting, and administrative services
    J. Financial management and an annual outside audit
    K. Liability and other business insurance
    L. Partnership administration (internal or external and who will do this work)
1. Payroll
2. Records
3. Benefits
4. Purchasing
5. Legal Services
    M. Three-year goals

III. Market analysis
(What needs do you want to serve? Is there a market for this, and how big is the market? Is there agreement with the governing board(s) on the target student population?)
    A. Parent, student, and governing board(s) Interest
    B. Student demographics
    C. Competitive analysis
1. What do governing boards and/or students and parents need?
2. How can those needs be met?
3. Who are we competing against?
    D. Target market

E.  Marketing/communication methods and tools
F.  Three-year enrollment estimates
IV. Learning program design and goals
(The learning program to be used in the educational environment where the TPP will operate. This may be for a single subject, for an on-line course, or for an entire school. The learning program may be created, or it may be chosen from programs developed by others.)
V.  Governing board relationship
(In each case the TPP will contract with a governing board to deliver service. What does the governing board want, and what are the respective roles? What reporting will be required?)
VI. School site operations and management plan
(Whether the TPP operates an entire school, a given subject in one or more schools, tutoring, or any other educational service, it will need an operations and management plan for that service. Some of the topics listed below apply most directly to a full school. However, most of them apply in all circumstances.)
A.  Organizational structure
B.  Staffing plan on a year-by-year basis
C.  Technology and systems
D.  Decision-making process
E.  Logistics
F.  Reporting
    1.  Governing board
    2.  State
    3.  Other
G.  Considerations for full school operations
    1.  Transportation
    2.  Security
    3.  Physical plant
    4.  Food service
    5.  Property and casualty insurance
VII. Three-year financial plan*
A.  Pro forma profit and loss statement
B.  Capital budget
C.  Cash flow statement

    D.  Balance sheet

    E.  Capitalization requirements

\* For suggested formats for the financial plan, see *Charter School Facilities: A Resource Guide on Development and Financing,* published by The National Cooperative Bank Development Corporation and Charter Friends Network. This is available free online at www.ncbdc.org. Also see *Small Business Resource Guide,* published by the Department of Treasury, Internal Revenue Service. This is available online at www.irs.gov.

# APPENDIX D

## Emerging Model: I.D.E.A.L. Charter School Cooperative

I.D.E.A.L. Charter School Cooperative (The Cooperative) of Milwaukee, Wisconsin, began operations in September 2001. The learning program it provides serves more than 200 children in a kindergarten for four-year-olds, a kindergarten for five-year-olds, and in grades 1–8. The Cooperative is formed under cooperative Wisconsin Statutes, Chapter 85, and is a 501 (c) 3 corporation under the Internal Revenue Code, that is, it is a nontaxable nonprofit organization. It operates to provide educational services to I.D.E.A.L. Charter School (The Charter School). Under Wisconsin law, The Charter School is not a separate legal entity. It is an instrumentality of the Milwaukee Public Schools (MPS). The Cooperative has a contract with MPS. While The Cooperative and The Charter School share part of the same name, they are not the same entities.

John Parr, the father of one of the founders and a consultant who works with labor unions, provided voluntary start-up assistance to the founders of The Cooperative. Parr realized quickly that while The Cooperative's founders wanted to design and manage their own learning program, they also desired to retain their participation in Wisconsin's public teacher retirement program. After some investigation, Parr discovered that retaining participation in the pension program requires the teachers to remain employees of MPS—but that they could get around having to adhere to MPS's standard learning program using some of the framework designed by EdVisions Cooperative in Minnesota.

With Parr's assistance, the founders designed a teacher professional partnership approach that would allow them to create and manage their own program while still participating in Wisconsin's public benefit structure. This TPP model allows The Charter School's teachers to remain MPS employees. Thus, they are able to continue as members of the teachers union, covered under the union's master contract. Accordingly, nonteacher employees of The Charter School are also MPS employees and members of their respective bargaining units. Retaining their status as MPS employees, the teachers and other employees continue to receive the same pension and other benefits negotiated by their bargaining units. Salaries will be those identified in the collective bargaining agreement. While using this structure means that the teachers may not experience all of the potential implications of ownership outlined in chapter 5, the teachers chose and defined this model because it most accurately fit their desires.

While The Cooperative is bound to the salary scale outlined in the master contract with the union, members are free to determine the number of teachers and other employees it will use to fulfill their separate contract with MPS to provide educational services at The Charter School. The Cooperative members also have the ability to choose the individual teachers who can become members, as well as who from that group will be their leaders. Under a memorandum of understanding with the teachers union and MPS, cooperative members will use a peer review system, which is a modification of the one required under the master contract, to evaluate teachers and determine whether they will continue as cooperative members. Should teachers choose to leave The Cooperative, they are still guaranteed jobs elsewhere in MPS.

The Charter School has a simple governance structure. It consists of a Parents Governance Board (PGB), made up of parents, students, teachers, and community members. The Cooperative operates through three committees. The Cooperative Finance Committee is made up of cooperative members and one member of the PGB. This committee presents a budget to the entire PGB for its approval. The PGB has final authority over the entire budget with the exception of the salaries, as specified in the master contract. The Cooperative also has a Personnel

Committee that includes one member of the PGB. This committee makes all personnel decisions. The Cooperative's Curriculum Committee is entirely made up of cooperative members. It determines the learning program and reports to the PGB once a year. MPS provides all administrative services. MPS makes an administrative charge allocation to cover all administrative expenses for The Charter School.

In summary, The Cooperative has control over and has accountability for the performance of the learning program. The members also determine the leaders, which teachers will be offered positions in The Charter School, as well as the culture, mission, vision, and values for The Cooperative. They do not control the budget, nor do they need to provide administrative services.

# APPENDIX E

## National Meeting on Teacher Professional Partnerships

The Center for Policy Studies, Hamline University, and Wallace-Readers Digest Funds cosponsored a meeting in September 2001 to discuss what happens when teachers are owners of their professional practice rather than employees. Participants discussed potential implications of the ownership model, as well as how several of the national discussions about teaching and teachers might change if the assumption of employment were removed and the questions were rethought on the assumption that teachers could be owners: the discussion about school leadership . . . about the improvement of learning and the change in teaching "practice" this might require . . . about compensation . . . about teacher supply and quality and training . . . about maximizing potential for new information technology. The meeting provided valuable insights, some of which have been incorporated into this guide. For this reason, we acknowledge the following participants in this discussion. The contents of the book remain the responsibility of the editor and steering committee that assisted in its formation.

**John S. Ayers**
Executive Director
Leadership for Quality Education

**Jon Bacal**
Director
SchoolStart

**Jim Bartholomew**
Education Policy Director
Minnesota Business Partnership

**Stacy Becker**
Independent Consultant
Center for Policy Studies

**Julie Blair**
Staff Writer
*Education Week*

**Bill Blazar**
Senior Vice President
Minnesota Chamber of Commerce

**Laura Bordelon**
Education Policy Manager
Minnesota Chamber of Commerce

**Robert J. Brown**
Professor, School of Education
University of Saint Thomas

**Elizabeth Bruch**
Dean, School of Education and
    Professional Development
Capella University

**Irving H. Buchen**
Senior Researcher
Center for School Renewal

**Lori Crouch**
Assistant Director
Education Writers Association

**Edward J. Dirkswager**
Associate
Center for Policy Studies

**Walter W. Enloe**
Associate Professor, School of
    Education
Hamline University

**Kimberly A. Farris**
Independent Consultant
Center for Policy Studies

**David Ferrero**
Program Officer
Bill & Melinda Gates Foundation

**Joseph P. Graba**
Senior Fellow
Hamline University

**Mindy Greiling**
Lead Democrat, K–12 Education
    Finance Committee
Minnesota House of
    Representatives

**Jerry Greiner**
Provost
Hamline University

**Susan Heegaard**
Independent Consultant
Center for Policy Studies

**Jennifer Henry**
Fellow
New Leaders for New Schools
    and The Chicago Academy

**Rose Hermodson**
Director, Government Relations
MN Department of Children,
    Families, and Learning

**Eric Hirsch**
Education Program Manager
National Conference of State
    Legislatures

**Ian Keith**
President
Saint Paul Federation of Teachers

**Barbara Kelley**
Chair
National Board for Professional
    Teaching Standards

**Edward Kirby**
The Walton Family Foundation

**Ted Kolderie**
Senior Associate
Center for Policy Studies

**Deirdre Kramer**
Interim Dean
Graduate School of Education
Hamline University

**Jane Krentz**
Education Committee and K–12
    Education Budget Division
Minnesota Senate

**Charles Kyte**
Executive Director
Minnesota Association of School
    Administrators

**Robert Lace**
Vice President
Saint Paul Federation of Teachers

**Harold K. Larson**
Former President, Board
    of Directors
EdVisions Cooperative

**Dan Loritz**
Vice President for University
    Relations
Hamline University

**Bruno Manno**
Senior Associate for Education
Annie E. Casey Foundation

**Thomas J. Marr**
Associate Medical Director
Health Partners

**John J. Mauriel**
Associate Professor, Carlson
    School of Management
University of Minnesota

**Ronald J. Newell**
Learning Program Director
Gates-EdVisions Project

**Michael Offerman**
President
Capella University

**John Parr**
President
John Parr Associates

**Steve Ramsey**
President
Ohio Charter Schools Association

**Jeremy Resnick**
Community Loan Fund of
  Southwestern Pennsylvania

**Jon Schnur**
Chief Executive Officer and
  Cofounder
New Leaders for New Schools

**Alice Seagren**
Chair, K–12 Education Finance
  Committee
Minnesota House of
  Representatives

**Louise Sundin**
President
Minneapolis Federation of Teachers

**Dee Grover Thomas**
Director
Minnesota New Country School/
  EdVisions Cooperative

**Douglas J. Thomas**
Director
Gates-EdVisions Project

**Thomas Toch**
Guest Scholar, Governmental
  Studies
The Brookings Institution

**Jeannie Ullrich**
Vice President
Edison College

*Panel of Teacher Owners:*

**Juan Figueroa**
El Colegio Charter School

**Bonnie Jean Flom**
EdVisions Consultant

**David Greenberg**
El Colegio
Charter School

**Dean Lind**
Minnesota New Country School

# APPENDIX F

# Technical Assistance: Where to Begin

## I. Starting a Small Business or Professional Partnership

**Internal Revenue Service (IRS)**
**Small Business and Self-Employed Community**
United States Department of the Treasury
1500 Pennsylvania Ave., NW
Washington, DC 20220
Phone: 202-622-2000      Fax: 202-622-6415
Web site: http://www.irs.gov/smallbiz/index.html

- Forms and Publications
- Electronic Filing
- Employment Tax Forms and Publications
- *Small Business Resource Guide*
  Provides critical tax information to small businesses including forms, instructions, and publications; valuable business information from a variety of government agencies, nonprofit organizations, and educational institutions; essential start-up information for new small businesses in order to be successful.
- New Business Resources & Starting a Business
- Contact Information for Local Small Business Experts

- Financing
- Links: American Express' *Small Business Network*; America On-line's *Government Guide*; and Microsoft's *bcentral*

**Library of Congress**
**Business Reference Services**
Science, Technology, and Business Division
Business Reference Services
Library of Congress
101 Independence Ave., SE
Washington, DC 20540-4754
Fax: 202-707-1925
E-mail: busref@loc.gov
Web site: http://lcweb.loc.gov/rr/business/

- Indexes, bibliographies, and guides including:
  *Entrepreneur's Reference Guide to Small Business Information* (getting started; raising capital; managing your business; human resources; marketing; doing business with government; research and information gathering; sources of statistics; handbooks and guides; etc.); and *Financing Small Business Enterprises* (overviews and sources for different types of financing; financial management for the small business; avoiding scams; etc.). Also includes guides to other business publications and source lists.

**Morebusiness.com**
**By Entrepreneurs, For Entrepreneurs**
Web site: http://www.Morebusiness.com

- Business how-tos: start a business (small business primer); incorporate; build your own web site; find funding now; market your products and services; manage your company and staff
- Templates: business and marketing plans; contracts and agreements; free legal forms; press releases; business checklists
- Tools: online financial calculators; business shareware; free intranet; free product and service quotes

## U.S. Small Business Administration Answer Desk
200 North College St., Suite A-2015
Charlotte, NC 28202
Phone: 1-800-UASK-SBA (1-800-827-5722)
E-mail: answerdesk@sba.gov
Web site: http://www.sba.gov/

- Starting Your Business: Success Series; First Steps; Start-up Kit; Research; Training
- Business Plans; State Resources (Workers' Compensation; Business Names, Licenses, or Incorporations; Tax Home Pages); Shareware
- Financing Your Business: Loan Programs; Loan Forms; Lending Programs; Lending Studies
- Loan Statistics; PRIME; Size Standards; Surety Bond; Secondary Market
- Offices and Services (descriptions of what SBA offers)
- Local Small Business Administration Offices
- Certification requirements
- Grant resources
- Online networks
- Small business classroom (digital strategy for training small business clients)
- Online library (Forms; Laws and Regulations; Listings and Directories; Publications)

**Other information on starting a small business of professional partnership can be found in the following documents:**

Clifford, Denis, and Ralph Warner. 2001, May. *The Partnership Book: How to Write a Partnership Agreement with CD-Rom.* Nolo.com publishing. This publication is a step-by-step guide about forming a partnership agreement.

Minars, David. 1997, September. *Partnerships Step-by-Step.* Barron's Education Series. This publication discusses how to form a partnership, property and rights of the parties, and financial obligations of each partner.

## II. Starting a Cooperative

**National Cooperative Bank**
1725 Eye St., NW, Suite 600
Washington, DC 20006
Phone: 800-955-9622; 202-336-7700      Fax: 202-336-7800
Web site: http://www.ncb.com/

**See also National Cooperative Bank Development Corporation**
        http://www.ncbdc.org/

- Co-op Basics: Co-ops 101 (Organizing and Operating a Coopera-
  tive); Benefits of Co-ops; Patronage and Taxation
- How to Start a Co-op (Laying the Groundwork; Determining Con-
  cept Feasibility; Forming the Cooperative Entity; Financing the
  Enterprise; Hiring Strong Management)
- Co-op Publications
- Real Estate
- Commercial and Small Business Lending
- Community Development
- Retail Banking
- Co-op Links

**National Cooperative Business Association**
1401 New York Ave., NW, Suite 1100
Washington, DC 20005
Phone: 202-638-6222      Fax: 202-638-1374
E-mail: ncba@ncba.org
Web site: http://www.ncba.org/index.cfm

- Co-op Catalog: Practical books and videos (How to Organize a Cooperative; Structure and Operations; Education for Board, Staff,
  and Members; Case Studies of Successes and Failures; Cooperative Finance and Credit Unions; Worker Cooperatives; History and
  Philosophy)
- Co-op Primer: Co-op Principles & Values, How to Start, Lessons
  for Success, Types & Structure, Historical Facts, Twin Pines Sym-
  bol, Statistics

- Buyer's Guide for Products and Services
- Cooperative Development
- Finance and Insurance: Credit Unions, Banks, Development Funds, Insurance Companies, Other Resources
- Co-op Links

**University of Wisconsin Center for Cooperatives (UWCC)**
230 Taylor Hall, 427 Lorch St.
Madison, WI 53706
Phone: 608-262-3981     Fax: 608-262-3251
E-mail: grinnell@aae.wisc.edu
Web site: http://www.wisc.edu/uwcc/index.html

- Information About Cooperatives: Community and Rural Development; Credit Unions/Banking; Electronic Commerce; Education and Training; Financial Management; Health Care and Insurance; Legal Issues; Management; Marketing; Media; Member Relations; Principles; Theory and History; Starting a Cooperative; Statistics; Cooperative Service Organizations; Current Cooperative News; Cooperative Theory and History
- Publications: Cooperative Development Update; Cooperative Journals and Periodicals; Rural
- Cooperative Publications; UWCC Staff Research and Publications; Others
- Co-op Links

**Gates-EdVisions Project**
Doug Thomas, Director
P.O. Box 518
501 Main St.
Henderson, MN 56044
Phone: 507-248-3738
E-mail: dthomas@mncs.k12.mn.us
Web site: http://www.edvisions.com

This site does not contain resources for starting a co-op, though it is a terrific example of a Web site representing a teacher cooperative. It describes the EdVisions Cooperative under the following subheadings: Vision for the Future; Services Provided; Biographical Information; Current Projects; Contact Information; Member School Contacts; Gates Foundation Information.

**Other information on starting a cooperative can be found in the following documents:**

*EdVisions Cooperative Comprehensive Guide: Scaling Up the Minnesota New Country School and Teacher Cooperative Ownership Models*. 2001. Gates-EdVisions Project.

Jackall, Robert, and Henry M. Levin, eds. 1984. *Worker Cooperatives in America.* Berkeley, CA: University of California at Berkeley.

## III. Starting a Charter School

**Center for Education Reform**
1001 Connecticut Ave., NW, Suite 204
Washington, DC 20036
Phone: 800-521-2118/202-822-9000        Fax: 202-822-5077
E-mail: cer@edreform.com
Web site: http://www.edreform.com/

- Introduction to Charter Schools: What Are Charter Schools; National and State Charter School Organizations and Resources; State Department of Education Charter School Contacts; Charter School Web Sites
- Charter School Laws, State by State
- *National Charter School Directory 2001–2*: Individual profiles and contact information on over 1,900 approved and operating charter schools around the nation, as well as the latest statistics, state by state, on schools, enrollment, grades served, sponsorship, and closures
- *The Charter School Workbook: Your Roadmap to the Charter School Movement*: A comprehensive but user-friendly resource on charter school issues from legislation and research to school successes and obstacles, to how-to and where-to-go
- Charter School Research Library

## Charter Schools Development Center
California State University Institute for Education Reform
6000 J St.
Foley Hall, Room 315
Sacramento, CA 95819-6018
Phone: 916-278-6069      Fax: 916-278-4094
E-mail: CSDC@calstate.edu
Web site: http://www.csus.edu/ier/charter/charter.html

- Start-up Resources: Charter School Development Guide; Charter School Development
- Workshop Materials; Charter Drafters' Tool Kit. These resources are specifically for California charter schools, but many of the tools are relevant to charter school start-up in any state.
- Resources for Charter Schools: Charter School Basics; Charter School Granting Agencies; Charter Law and Policy; Curriculum and Instruction; Staffing and Labor Relations; Charter School News; Starting a Charter School; Standards, Assessment, and Accountability; Charter School Finance; Charter Links
- Charter School Grants
- Studies and Research
- *Charter Pages* School Directory

## U.S. Department of Education
400 Maryland Ave., SW
Washington, DC 20202-0498
Phone: 1-800-USA-LEARN (1-800-872-5327)
Web site: www.uscharterschools.org

- Start-up and Assistance: Steps to Starting a Charter School; Case Study of a Charter School; Developing a Mission Statement; Accountability: Standards, Assessment, & Using Data; Budget, Finance, & Fundraising; Educational Program Design; Facilities; Family-Friendly Charter Schools; Governing Boards; Human Resources; Staffing for Success; Special Education Resources; Information for Charter Authorizers

- State and School Information: Charter Community Online Exchange (to interact with colleagues); Profiles of Schools; Discussion Groups; Legislative summaries; Key State-Level Contacts
- Resources: Sample documents from schools and authorizers; funding opportunities; service providers; reports and research
- Technical Assistance Documents: Illinois Charter School Developer's Handbook; Getting Your Charter School off the Ground; "Charter School Governance Toolkit"; "Shaping Positive Cultures in Charter Schools"; "Faculty Performance Evaluation Form"; Sample Teacher Evaluation Process; and Others
- Federal Resources: Federal funding; research; guidance

**Charter Friends National Network**
1745 University Ave., Suite 110
Saint Paul, MN 55104
E-mail: info@charterfriends.org
Web site: http://www.charterfriends.org

- State-by-State Directory of Charter-Support Organizations and Activities
- Technical Assistance Materials/Publications
- Charter Friends Initiatives: Accountability; Facilities Financing; Special Education; Federal Policy Development
- Writings on Education Policy

**Charter Friends National Network (CFNN) has published a number of resource guides that are available on CFNN's Web site or may be requested by contacting CFNN at jon@charterfriends.org. Current CFNN resource guides include:**

*A Guide for Developing a Business Plan for Charter Schools* (1998, February). This publication offers practical suggestions and outline and sample budgets that can be used by charter developers in preparing a business plan to be included with a charter application and with grant and loan requests.

*Making Matches that Make Sense: A Report on Opportunities and Obstacles to Forging Links Between Charter Schools and Comprehensive*

*School Design Programs* (1998, May). This report identifies and analyzes the major challenges that inhibit links between charters and school design groups and offers recommendations for a number of strategies that can be used to address those challenges.

*Accountability for Student Performance—An Annotated Resource Guide for Shaping an Accountability Plan for Your Charter School* (1998, June). This resource guide offers dozens of resources grouped under six key questions schools need to ask and answer as they develop accountability plans that match their unique missions and goals.

*If the Shoe Fits! A Guide for Charter Schools Thinking about a Pre-existing Comprehensive School Design* (1998, August). This resource guide is designed for charters to use in deciding whether a partnership with a school design group could be in their interest and offers some helpful hints for evaluating individual school designs to determine if there might be a mutually beneficial fit.

*Paying for the Charter Schoolhouse* (1999, February). This twenty-two-page resource guide contains both policy options and examples of current initiatives to use public financing and public/private partnerships to help meet the facilities needs of charter schools.

*Out of the Box: An Idea Book on Charter School Facilities Financing* (1999, June). This publication aims to help charter school leaders identify creative ways to finance facilities, drawing on the real-life experiences of dozens of charter schools around the country.

*Charting a Clear Course: A Resource Guide for Charter Schools Contracting with School Management Organizations* (2001, April). This publication raises common issues that have arisen in contracting arrangements, noting important considerations and options for both parties. It includes examples from existing contracts on key issues like roles and responsibilities of charter boards, performance evaluation, and compensation.

*Charter School Facilities: A Resource Guide on Development and Financing* (2000, April). CFNN and the National Cooperative Bank Development Corporation have collaborated on this guide that walks charter school operators through all the major steps of facility planning, development, and financing.

*Employer-Linked Charter Schools: An Introduction* (2000, June). Produced jointly by Public Policy Associates, CFNN, and the National Alliance, this guide includes profiles on employer-linked charters as well as experience and advice from successfully operating schools on how to form employer–charter school partnerships.

*Charter Schools and Special Education: A Guide for Navigating the Challenges and Opportunities of Serving Students with Disabilities* (2001, April). The second edition of a pioneering work on special education and charter schools that was originally produced in 1997 by Project FORUM at the National Association of State Directors of Special Education.

*Creating an Effective Charter School Governing Board* (2000, December). Produced in partnership with the Annie E. Casey Foundation, this guide offers strategic advice for meeting twelve critical challenges that charter school governing boards must meet.

*Personnel Policies and Practices: Understanding Employment Law* (2000, December). Produced in partnership with the Annie E. Casey Foundation, this guide is designed to help charters develop basic personnel policies that meet all federal, state, and local regulations and law.

*Creating and Sustaining Family Friendly Charter Schools* (2000, December). Produced in partnership with the Annie E. Casey Foundation, this guide helps charter founders develop schools that are connected to their communities and both involve and serve families whose children attend them.

*Mobilizing and Motivating Staff to Get Results* (2000, December). Produced in partnership with the Annie E. Casey Foundation, this guide is designed to help charters think creatively about their use of compensation and benefits, recruitment, selection, professional development, staff organization, and performance evaluation to best serve their schools.

*Partnering with Community-Based Organizations* (2001, Summer). Produced in partnership with the Annie E. Casey Foundation, this guide will focus on lessons learned and best practices in starting and operating charter schools in partnership with established community-based organizations.

*Charter School Facilities* (2001, April). Produced in partnership sixteen, this report documents the results of the first-ever national survey of charter schools, documenting their facilities needs and current arrangements.

# BIBLIOGRAPHY

Bacal, Jon. 2001 (April 23). Conversation with Pete Hovde (Avalon School Board Chair).

Brandt, Ron. 1998. *Assessing Student Learning: New Rules, New Realities*. Arlington, Va.: Educational Research Service.

Caine, Renate Nummela, and Geoffrey Caine. 1997. *Unleashing the Power of Perceptual Change: The Potential of Brain-Based Teaching*. Alexandria, Va.: Association for Supervision and Curriculum.

*Charter School Facilities: A Resource Guide on Development and Financing*. 2000. Washington, DC: National Cooperative Bank Development Corporation and Charter Friends National Network, http://www.ncbdc.org [accessed 25 Jul. 2001].

*Charting a Clear Course: A Resource Guide for Charter Schools Contracting with School Management Organizations*. Second Edition. 2001. Saint Paul, Minn.: Charter Friends National Network, http://www.charterfriends.org/contract.pdf [accessed 25 July 2001].

Christensen, Clayton M. 2000. *Innovator's Dilemma: The Revolutionary National Bestseller That Changed the Way We Do Business*. New York: HarperBusiness.

Cohen, Jonathan, ed. 1999. *Educating Minds and Hearts: Social Emotional Learning and the Passage into Adolescence*. New York: Teachers College Press.

Collary, Michelle, Diane Dunlap, Walter Enloe, and George Gagnon. 1998. *Learning Circles: Creating Conditions for Professional Development*. Thousand Oaks, Calif.: Corwin Press.

*Creating an Effective Charter School Governing Board.* 2000. Saint Paul, Minn: Charter Friends National Network, http://www.uscharterschools.org/gb/governance [accessed 25 July 2001].

Cuban, Larry. 1984. *How Teachers Taught: Constancy and Change in American Classrooms 1890–1984.* New York: Longman Press.

———. 1990. "Reforming Again, Again, and Again." *Educational Researcher*: 19:3–13.

Elmore, Richard. 1996. "Getting to Scale with Successful Educational Practices." In *Rewards and Reform: Creating Educational Incentives That Work*, Susan H. Fuhrman and Jennifer A. O'Day, eds. San Francisco: Jossey-Bass, p. 295.

Eurich, Nell. 1990. *The Learning Industry: Education for Adult Workers.* Princeton, N.J.: Carnegie Foundation for the Advancement of Teaching.

Evans, Robert. 2001. *The Human Side of School Change: Reform, Resistance, and the Real-Life Problems of Innovation.* San Franscisco: Jossey-Bass.

Farkas, Steve, Patrick Foley, Ann Duffett, Tony Foleno, and Jean Johnson. 2001. "Just Waiting to Be Asked? A Fresh Look at Attitudes on Public Engagement." *Public Agenda Online: The Inside Source for Public Opinion and Policy Analysis* [online]. New York: Public Agenda, http://www.publicagenda.org/specials/pubengage/pubengage.htm [cited 25 July 2001].

Fogel, Daniel S. 1990. "The Uniqueness of a Professionally Dominated Organization." *Health Care Management Review* 14: 15–24.

Foster, Richard, and Sarah Kaplan. 2001. *Creative Destruction: Why Companies That Are Built to Last Underperform the Market—And How to Successfully Transform Them.* New York: Doubleday.

*Fundamentals of School Board Membership: A Guide for Newly Elected Charter School Board Members.* 1998. St. Peter, Minn.: Minnesota School Boards Association.

Geldens, Max. 1984 (June 28). "How to Get Jobs." *The Economist*, 19–22.

Hill, Paul T. 2001. "Charter School Districts." *Progressive Policy Institute* [online]. Washington, DC: Progressive Policy Institute, http://www.ppionline.org/ppi_ci.cfm?contented=3365&knlgAreaID=11-&subsecid=134 [accessed 26 July 2001].

Hill, Paul T., Lawrence C. Pierce, and James W. Guthrie. 1997 © *Reinventing Public Education: How Contracting Can Transform America's Schools.* Chicago: University of Chicago Press.

Hirschman, Albert O. 1970. *Exit, Voice and Loyalty: Responses to Decline in Firms, Organizations and States.* Boston, Mass.: Harvard University Press, p. 125.

Kohn, Jennifer, and Sandy Baird. 1999–2001. "Company Overview." *Tutor.com: Real Tutors. Real Results* [online]. New York: Tutor.com, Inc., http://www.tutor.com/press/Company_overview.pdf [accessed 25 July 2001].

Kolderie, Ted. G. 1984 (May 30). Discussion convened by Minnesota Business Partnership in which Arley Gunderman participated.

———. 1984 (June 23). Conversation with Alan K. Campbell.

———. 1986. *Private Practice in Public School Teaching. Book I: The Concept, Need and Design.* Minneapolis, Minn.: Public School Incentives.

———. 1988 (October). Conversation with Albert Shanker.

———. Conversation with Bill Ridley.

———. Conversation reported to Ted Kolderie by Frank Newman (former president of Education Commission of the States).

Kusy, Mitchell, Louellen Essex, and Thomas Marr. 1995. "No Longer a Solo Practice: How Physician Leaders Lead." *The Physician Executive* 21: 11–15.

Marr, Thomas J., and Daniel K. Zismer. 1998. "When Is a Physician Network a Group?" *The Physician Executive* 24: 25–29.

*Minnesota New Country School Seventh Annual Report.* 2000 (September 15) Henderson, Minn.: EdVisions Cooperative.

Murphy, John, and Dennis Doyle. 2001. "Redesigning the Operating Environments in School Districts and Schools." *ECS Governance Notes* [online]. Denver, Colo.: Education Commission of the States, http://www.ecs.org/ecsmain.asp?page=/html/newsMedia/governancenotes.asp [accessed 25 July 2001].

National Commission on Governing America's Schools. 1999. "Governing America's Schools: Changing the Rules" [online] Denver, Colo.: Education Commission of the States, www.ecs.org [accessed 25 July 2001].

Newell, Ron. 2001 (July 7–8) Conversation with Dee Grover Thomas.

Olson, Ruth Anne. 1986. *Private Practice in Public School Teaching. Book II: The Experiences of Teachers and School Administrators.* Minneapolis, Minn.: Public School Incentives.

Reason, Peter, and Harold Bradbury. 2001. *Handbook of Action Research: Participative Inquiry and Practice.* London: Sage Publishing.

Quinn, James, Phillip Anderson, and Sydney Finkelstein. 1996 (March–April). "Managing Professional Intellect: Making the Most of the Best." *Harvard Business Review* 71–80.

*Small Business Resource Guide.* 2001. Washington, DC: Department of Treasury, Internal Revenue Service, and Small Business Administration, http://www.irs.gov/prod/bus_info/sm_bus/smbus-cd.html [accessed 25 July 2001].

Thomas, Doug. 1996. *Professional Development Checklist.* Henderson, Minn.: EdVisions Cooperative.

# ABOUT THE EDITOR AND CONTRIBUTORS

All of the individuals who have contributed to this book have experience in professional practice organizations and/or education policy or practice. They are lawyers, physicians, accountants, consultants, persons familiar with small businesses and cooperatives, educators, education policymakers, and educational administrators.

**Edward J. Dirkswager**, the editor, is an associate at the Center for Policy Studies, St. Paul, Minnesota. He was a health care business executive and consultant with long-term involvement in public education. He worked on a task force of the Minnesota Business Partnership that recommended the legislative enactment allowing students freedom of choice among public schools. He has been a member of a professional partnership and has helped others to start many new for-profit and nonprofit organizations and partnerships.

**Ted Kolderie**, the author of the foreword, is senior associate at the Center for Policy Studies. He is recognized nationwide for his work on education policy and innovation. He has worked on state and local public policy issues in Minnesota since 1956 and on public education almost continuously since 1983. Kolderie was instrumental in helping to design and pass the nation's first charter school law and has worked on charter school legislation in over seventeen states.

Other contributors are: Jon Bacal, director, SchoolStart; Stacy Becker, Becker Consulting; Robert J. Brown, professor of education, University of St. Thomas; Walter W. Enloe, associate professor of education, Hamline University; Kimberly A. Farris, Farris Consulting; Thomas W. Garton, partner, Fredrickson & Byron; Allen Gerber, executive director, Southeast Service Cooperative; Joseph P. Graba, senior policy fellow and former dean of the Graduate School of Education at Hamline University; Harold K. Larson, former superintendent, Le Sueur-Henderson School District; Thomas J. Marr, associate medical director, HealthPartners; John J. Mauriel, associate professor, Carlson School of Management; Daniel C. Mott, partner, Oppenheimer Wolff & Donnelly LLP; Ronald J. Newell, Learning Program director, Gates-EdVisions Project; Al Oukrop, consultant to cooperatives; Douglas J. Thomas, director, Gates-EdVisions Project; and James R. Walker, former superintendent, North Branch School District.